Rock Climbing
Minnesota and
Wisconsin

Mike Farris

FALCONGUIDE®

GUILFORD, CONNECTICUT
HELENA, MONTANA
AN IMPRINT OF THE GLOBE PEQUOT PRESS

A FALCON GUIDE®

Black-and-white photos by Mike Farris unless otherwise noted.

Front cover: Climbing on the North Shore of Lake Superior, Minnesota. Photo by Richard Hamilton Smith.
Back cover: Caren Reich on Upper Diagonal, Devil's Lake, Wisconsin. Photo by Dave Reich.

Library of Congress Cataloging-in-Publication Data

Farris, Mike, 1955–
   Rock Climbing Minnesota and Wisconsin / Mike Farris.
       p. cm.
   ISBN-13: 978-1-56044-984-3
   ISBN-10: 1-56044-984-5
   1. Rock climbing--Minnesota--Guidebooks. 2. Rock
   climbing--Wisconsin--Guidebooks. 3. Minnesota--Guidebooks. 4.
   Wisconsin--Guidebooks. 1. Title.

   GV199.42.M6 F37 2000
   796.52'23'09775--dc21   00-037674

Manufactured in Canada
First Edition/Second Printing

CONTENTS

PREFACE

When I moved from Boulder, Colorado, to Minnesota in 1985 I figured that my opportunities to climb would be few and far between. Much to my delight, I found that Minnesota and Wisconsin harbor the best climbing west of Seneca and east of Boulder and that the variety and quality of rock here are surprisingly good.

Writing a climbing guide used to be pretty easy; climb the routes and write them up. At the turn of the new century, two related issues are just as important: access and the influx of undertrained climbers. Cliffs in the Midwest lie almost exclusively on state, county, or private lands. Each has its own set of access issues, and often we must deal with officials who lack the expertise to deal with climbing. In areas that allow climbing, future access is not necessarily assured. This guide is an attempt to get the best available access information to you.

I have written the text for the vast number of newer climbers out there who lack experienced companions to learn from. I've not been subtle about safety or access issues, and I apologize in advance if I seem to overstress these points. This is not an instructional book, but I hope that these climbers will learn a little as they use this guide. Indoor climbing is a very controlled, nearly risk-free activity that represents only a portion of the climbing experience. The climbs described here have more potential dangers—and far greater rewards.

I have tried to give you enough information to find each route and a general idea of what to expect when you climb it. I have tried to preserve the need for routefinding skills, good judgment, and commitment. I have not climbed every route in this guide, and some of the ratings are based on ancient information.

My previous selected climbs guide mostly covered areas whose guidebooks were out of print. I hoped that some enterprising folks would take up the challenge to produce comprehensive guides to these areas, but as of this writing that has not happened. As a result, I've generally tried to provide complete coverage for crags not currently blessed with a guidebook. Boulder problems are generally not included; they deserve to be covered by a passionate boulderer.

You might ask, "What's a guidebook photographer's most important piece of equipment?" The answer (in the Midwest anyway) is a chainsaw. Ansel Adams may disagree, but taking a decent photo of El Capitan is trivial compared to getting a clear shot of a black, north-facing crag rising out of a birch forest. I've tried to provide the best shots possible given the limitations of each site. Many pictures were by necessity taken with a 24mm lens, which distorts the apparent angle of the rock (especially in horizontal shots). Most of the pictures were taken under cloudy conditions to eliminate tree shadows. You will also notice a complete lack of topos. This is because 1) the typical topo cannot provide the detail found in a decent photo and 2) I can't draw.

Do me a favor. I can't improve this guide if I don't know what's wrong with it. Tell me about any new routes, bad ratings or descriptions, or any other problem you have with this guide. Contact Mike Farris, c/o Falcon Publishing, Inc., PO Box 1718, Helena, Montana 59624.

The folks at Falcon Publishing deserve the credit for getting this project going and finishing it successfully. John Burbidge has guided this guide throughout and I appreciate all of his hard work. To those who transformed the endless photos and crude maps into the images in this guide, thank you.

The following climbers and land managers contributed in various ways to this guide. I have included in this list those folks who helped mightily with the first edition, as their input is still alive in this guide. For their help, I would like to thank Tom Anderson, Keith Anderson, Stephen Anderson, Alex Andrews, Scott Backes, Jim Bjork, Ed Burrell, Len Crowley, Steve Frykman, Steve Gilmore, Jim Hunter, Todd Johnson, Eric Landmann, Michelle Lewis, Andrzej Malewicz, Dave McConnell, Dave McKay, Bob Myers, Dave Pagel, Kay Pitkin, Nate Postma, Stephen Regenold, Dave Reich, Peter Smerud, Tak Tang, Steve Vernstrom, Mona Vernstrom, John Wanner, and Rick White. This guide would also not be possible without the efforts of previous guidebook writers.

Several folks deserve special mention. Phil Leversedge, Tettegouche State Park manager, provided the current Minnesota Climbing Management Plan and helped procure the pictures of Palisade Head. Jeff Engel and Paul Bjork deserve mention for their efforts to establish climbing access at Willow River; much of the information in this guide came from Jeff's mini-guide to that area. Josh Helke helped considerably with both Red Wing and Willow River.

Mike Dahlberg spent hours improving numerous sections of this guide. His input on the Taylors Falls chapter was invaluable. My climbing partners, Bruce McDonald and David Dahl, have willingly thrashed through the brush in search of mossy old climbs for the last year or so; you guys get to pick where we climb for a while. My son David used his skills as a geologist to make more sense of the jumbled geologic history of this region than I ever could. Finally, my wife Kathy has contributed in immeasurable ways with this guide and has endured much as I've struggled with this project.

—*Mike Farris*
Northfield, MN
October 1999

Flocks of birds have flown high and away.
A solitary drift of cloud, too, has gone, wandering on.
And I sit alone with the Chang-Ting Peak, towering beyond.
We never grow tired of each other, the mountain and I.

—Li Po (d. 762)

MAP LEGEND

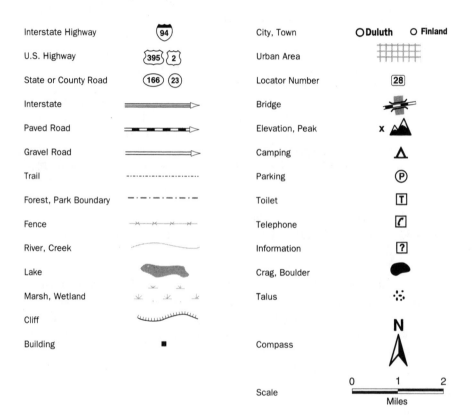

Interstate Highway	94	City, Town	○ Duluth	○ Finland
U.S. Highway	395 2	Urban Area		
State or County Road	166 23	Locator Number	28	
Interstate		Bridge		
Paved Road		Elevation, Peak	x	
Gravel Road		Camping	△	
Trail		Parking	℗	
Forest, Park Boundary		Toilet	T	
Fence		Telephone		
River, Creek		Information	?	
Lake		Crag, Boulder		
Marsh, Wetland		Talus		
Cliff				
Building	■	Compass	N	
		Scale	0 1 2 Miles	

MINNESOTA AND WISCONSIN CLIMBING AREAS

1 Blue Mounds
2 Devil's Lake
3 Red Wing
4 Willow River
5 Taylors Falls
6 Elys Peak
7 Palisade Head and Shovel Point
8 Mystical Mountain Zone
9 Carlton Peak

Introduction

We are entering a new era of climbing, an era that may well be characterized by . . . the rendering of the mountains to a low, though democratic mean. Or it could be the start of more spiritual climbing, where we assault the mountains with less equipment and with more awareness, more experience and more courage.

—Yvon Chouinard

ACCESS

Climbers are now overwhelming many of our favorite crags. As we move toward a new millennium, our greatest challenge may not be pushing the limits of technical difficulty, but instead may be retaining the right to climb in areas that have traditionally been used by a far smaller number of climbers. One of our major tasks as climbers is maintaining our freedom of personal expression while sustaining the health of the ecological systems that we use.

Climbing closures are taking place with alarming regularity and some very good climbs that would have been in this book are now out of bounds or can't be published. On both a national and regional level, many of these access problems are a result of the misplaced fears of landowners, but some closures have been caused by the inappropriate activities of climbers. **It is the responsibility of every climber to preserve the ecological, geological and aesthetic qualities of the climbing environment for future users.**

This simple rule serves as the ultimate touchstone for judging any activity related to climbing, and continues a tradition of respect for the land that has been held by climbers for centuries. Fortunately, indoor walls now provide an outlet for those individuals who must walk over nature and not with it.

There are a lot of sandstone cliffs in the Driftless Area and along river valleys. I have chosen not to cover these areas in this guide due to uncertain access, especially in Wisconsin. It is imperative that climbers wishing to use these areas put in the hard work needed to secure legal permission to climb there. It is also imperative that those visiting those areas practice a "leave no trace" philosophy—most importantly that means "leave no bolts" if access is unclear. There is little to be gained and much to be lost if landowners find that climbers are significantly altering the landscape without permission.

Join The Access Fund, and get involved. Join local access organizations, such as the Wisconsin Outdoor Access, or WOA (see Appendix A), and get involved.

Tarek Haddad on Dance of the Sugar Plum Fairies, *Shovel Point, North Shore of Lake Superior.*

Pay park entry fees, and get on the climbing advisory board for your local park. Make comments on management plans. Help clarify access on that one little crag in the park down the road. It's up to you.

THE MINNESOTA STATE CLIMBING MANAGEMENT PLAN

In 1995 the Minnesota State Parks system developed a management plan to deal with climbing within the park system. I have reprinted the opening section of the CMP in Appendix C, omitting only the definitions (which climbers are familiar with). Sections specific to each park are included in that section of the guide.

THE WISCONSIN STATE CLIMBING MANAGEMENT PLAN

Wisconsin is currently developing a CMP for lands administered by the Wisconsin Department of Natural Resources. There is no finalized plan at this time. Ask at Wisconsin State Park offices to obtain a copy of the plan when it is finalized.

ENVIRONMENTAL ETHICS

Many climbing areas are being loved to death. Rock is relatively resistant to our assaults, but the biological environment is far more delicate. Clifton Gorge, a nifty little dolomite crag in Ohio, is now closed to climbing primarily because of damage to the cliff ecosystem caused by climbers. Closer to home, The Cross Area at Taylors Falls is closed due to erosion damage caused in part by climbers.

Many pages could be devoted to defining environmental damage and the relative impacts of different climbing activities. While some aspects of climbing may damage the environment in obvious ways, other practices aren't so clear. Bolting at Red Wing is an example. While the bolts permanently damage the rock (in this case, an old quarry), they also prevent excessive top-roping. The loose loess that caps Barn Bluff would suffer tremendous damage via trampling if the same number of climbers top-roped all of these climbs—and many people would get hurt due to falling debris.

The future of climbing in most areas in this guide depends on climbers, as a group, cooperating with those who own and administer the cliffs we need for our sport. The most important actions you can take are to:

- Pay park entry fees and park in appropriate spots.

- Register as a climber if requested.

- Stay on developed trails, or on logically located unofficial paths. Don't take shortcuts.

- Walk on rocks or root tops, not soil, at the bases and tops of cliffs.

- Minimize the use of chalk (of any color); avoid chalk if local ethics prohibit it.

- Do not place pitons or bolts; do not chip or glue rock holds.

- Avoid "cleaning" (destroying vegetation, including lichens).

- Pick up all of your litter (including cigarette butts) and a little bit more.

TREES

Every time you anchor to a tree, you enter The Death Zone. Not *your* death zone, but the delicate region of soil that contains the roots which keep the tree anchored and fed. Trees in cliff habitats often have very little soil in which to live, and erosion caused by trampling is likely to cause more tree deaths than the wear and tear generated by slings. Erosion is currently most severe at Taylors Falls, while Shovel Point and Palisade Head are the most likely cliffs to suffer a major loss of trees in the future.

Climbers can preserve trees by taking a few simple precautions. First, don't walk on soil found underneath the crown of the tree, since this zone contains most of the roots. Instead, stand on rocks or even large, exposed roots. Second, when tying into a tree, try to approach the tree without breaking any branches. Third, test the tree for stability before using it. Birches are untrustworthy, and along the North Shore apparently solid large conifers can often be easily rocked back and forth due to the thin soil.

SAFETY

> "Ay, it's a good life," he mused, "providing you don't weaken."
> "What happens if you do?"
> "They bury you," he growled, and finished his pint.
> —TOM PATEY, *A Short Walk with Whillans*

Midwestern crags seem relatively benign when compared to the alpine climbs a day's drive to our west. There are a number of potential problems that may trap the unwary, however, and some of these are listed below. If you want to read more of this sort of cheery stuff, check out the section entitled *Staying Alive* in the Yosemite guidebooks or pick up the latest copy of *Accidents in North American Mountaineering* at your local climbing shop. Experience is no protection against accidents, so keep your guard up regardless of your aptitude. While some people feel that there are climbs worth dying for, it's certain that none of them are in the Midwest.

Your attitude. Your own outlook will determine your safety in almost every situation. All climbers are ultimately responsible for themselves, and even the first-time climber needs to take personal responsibility for his or her own safety. Do not count on your partner, your friends, your spouse, your instructor, or bystanders to keep you healthy. If something seems wrong, stop, ask questions, and don't proceed until you are completely satisfied. Once in a while you just might have a strong impulse to avoid a particular climb or take the day off. Listen to those little voices.

Loose rock. The rock is intrinsically solid at all areas in this guide except for Red Wing, Willow River, and to a lesser extent, Palisade Head. However, all cliffs are losing the constant battle with erosion, and both loose rock and falling rock may be experienced at any crag. This is especially true in the spring, when both big and little rocks have been loosened by freeze-thaw action. Any gully or low-angle area that you find on an otherwise steep cliff is usually a natural rockfall area; the *Jammermeister* gully at Taylors Falls, the *Leaning Tower Gully* at Devil's Lake, and *Southern Escape Gully* at Palisade Head are examples.

Tourists. Non-climbers congregate at the tops of many cliffs and pose a hazard. Kids of all ages feel compelled to drop things (and occasionally themselves) over the edge, even though you are clearly visible below. They also are fascinated by climbing gear and may not understand that tampering with the anchoring system may lead to an involuntary manslaughter charge. They also like to get drunk and break bottles on the climbs and approaches, though this seems to be less of a problem now than in previous years.

Fixed protection. Bolts and fixed pitons are common to nonexistent, depending on the area. As John Long says, the term "fixed" means "stuck," not "capable of holding a fall." Pitons should always be considered unreliable. A fellow cratered at Carlton Peak in 1993 because he forgot this rule. The trouble with bolts is that there is no way to test their integrity once they are placed. Even the most carefully placed bolt is only as strong as the rock in which it is found. Never hammer on a bolt to test it!

Never trust your life to a single anchor point. Three Minnesota climbers died on El Capitan in 1977 in a widely publicized accident involving fixed protection failure. Two bolts were chained together, and they apparently passed the rope over the *top* of the chain. One bolt failed, and if you can't figure out what happened next, don't be setting up any anchor systems on your own!

At Red Wing, many of the cold shuts and anchor carabiners at the chains are of first ascent vintage and need to be replaced. If every climber would replace just one worn anchor. . . .

Rappelling. This is a skill that every climber should master, but good climbers regard it as a necessary evil and not as a cheap thrill. There are just too many ways to get the chop while rappelling: anchor failure, rockfall, and accidental disconnection from the rope or anchors, to name a few.

If you absolutely must rappel on these cliffs, avoid popular climbs and areas of loose rock. Consider providing a real belay for neophytes—don't just hold the rope at the bottom. Resist the urge to bounce or jump, as this may overload the anchors or cut the rope on an edge. Leave the fancy techniques to the military since there is no call for a no-hands, head-first rappel in peacetime climbing (besides, everyone will assume that you're a weenie). Never run the rope around trees, and never pull such a rope down from below, as you can kill the tree.

Leading. Learning to lead in the Midwest is great training for climbing slowly. Most climbs are fairly steep and continuous, and the aspiring leader usually ends up placing a lot of possibly marginal protection because of the chance of a groundfall. This practice, when transferred to longer climbs elsewhere, has led to many involuntary bivouacs (ask me, I know).

Though many climbers put in lots of gear when leading, inadequate protection is a major contributor to longer-than-necessary leader falls. There are three reasons for this problem. First, many climbers (especially new leaders) are trying to lead right at the edge of their technical ability and expect to take a lot of leader falls (gym climber syndrome); more falling means a greater chance of injury. Second, spring-loaded camming devices (Friends, Camalots, etc.) are easy to place incorrectly, especially if you are in a tenuous position. Finally, many climbers use very short slings (quickdraws) on every piece they place. These short slings can lever out even a great placement and lead to a longer fall than would have occurred if a full-length runner were used.

As you learn to lead, evaluate the protection factor along with the technical difficulty before you attempt the climb. By learning to lead on climbs that do not challenge your technical ability, you can develop your protection skills in a less threatening situation. Have an experienced leader check your placements and evaluate your entire system after you lead. Another option is to do some top-roped leading to learn how to place protection on harder climbs.

Most of the routes in this guide have been led. I have included a list of commonly led routes at most areas, routes with reasonable protection when climbed by a competent leader (it's your responsibility to determine your competence). Most routes can be seen from the ground, so evaluate the protection potential on your own. All leaders should watch out for well-worn, slippery rock at Taylors Falls, Devil's Lake, and Blue Mounds, as well as loose rock (especially at Red Wing and Palisade Head).

Sharing top-ropes. Sharing top-ropes has been a common practice, but I've quit bumming rides unless I check out the setup first. I once saw a fellow fall at the bottom of a climb, and as he weighted the rope the anchor failed. Apparently, the rope was anchored with a single sling around a large tree and the knot became untied. Don't assume anything!

Top-rope setups. Your top-rope setup may need to withstand dozens of minor falls, abrasion over sharp edges, numerous pendulums, and the prodding of curious tourists. Here are a number of things to keep in mind:

- Each individual component of the anchor system must always have a backup. Passing the rope through a single locking carabiner is not sufficient; use two or three carabiners with gates opposed and reversed.
- At least three independent anchors should be attached to the carabiners anchoring the rope (preferably in at least two separate crack systems).
- Avoid using small stoppers and camming devices (especially TCUs) as anchors; they are often neither strong nor secure. Nuts are more difficult than cams to dislodge (and cheaper to replace).
- Avoid tying into trees of any size when possible. A proper tie-in will not damage the tree, but many trees are dying due to the abuse of climbers (see above). If you insist, use webbing and not rope for your anchor, and pad the tree for the most protection. Cedars and junipers have relatively thin bark and are especially prone to damage. Avoid loosely rooted trees and trees smaller than six inches in diameter.
- Equalize your anchors to pass the load to all of them. Keep the slings passing over the edge from sawing side-to-side by locating your anchors properly. Pad any sharp edges as necessary.
- Make sure the carabiners anchoring the rope hang far enough over the edge to prevent rope abrasion. Again, pad rock edges as needed.
- Make sure an adequate anchor is available for the belayer. When belaying from above, this anchor must be as bombproof as a top-rope anchor, and there can be no slack in the system.
- Do a complete check of all portions of the system when you're finished with the setup and recheck the setup periodically throughout the day.

To new climbers and gym climbers. If you are new to climbing, or if you started climbing indoors and now wish to move outside, here are a few suggestions that may help you survive the transition. If you are still reading, half of the battle is already won, because you understand that you have a lot more to learn.

- Nobody is maintaining the cliffs for you as they do at the gym. The rocks are loose (maybe), the bolts are bad (maybe), the ratings are different (probably), and nobody is watching over you.

- You can't safely top-rope with a handful of webbing and a couple of carabiners. You can top-rope just about anything if you add a set of hexes and stoppers and a few more carabiners.

- The best way to learn to set good protection is to clean gear placed by good climbers.

- Your equipment is your life–buy it from a trusted source. You won't find substandard new climbing gear for sale, but some stores do not have climbers on staff to help you choose the gear that best suits your needs. As a newer climber, only buy gear at shops where experienced climbers are available to help you make the right choices. Don't be afraid to ask the clerks about their experience when they recommend equipment to you.

- Using a guide or instructor? Be darned sure s/he is well qualified. As a rule of thumb, anyone with less than five years of solid outdoor climbing experience is unlikely to have encountered enough different situations to allow them to safely teach others. Watch out for individuals that are excited about rappelling, use military techniques and equipment, or have recently taken climbing classes. A good instructor will appreciate your interest in her/his qualifications, safety procedures, etc. Ask where your guide has climbed, what s/he has recently led, or if s/he has been involved in any climbing accidents. If appropriate answers aren't forthcoming, go somewhere else to learn.

As I hang from my harness, I recall the overwhelming indifference of
El Capitan. Toward the three boys from Minnesota. Toward us. I know
this bears remembering, and I eye the anchors again and again.
I am ready.
—DICK SHOCKLEY, *Cruising Up the Salathé Wall*

STYLE AND ETHICS

People climb for many different reasons. More and more people seem to be attracted to the purely physical aspects of climbing rather than the aesthetic or exploratory aspects. As a result, you find yourself on the crags with a very diverse group of people. Some are there for the sunshine, some for the companionship, some for the competition, and some due to peer pressure. Different motivations lead to different styles.

In the cosmic sense, you can climb however you want as long as you don't cause environmental damage. However, the quality of your ascents can and should be measured by the style that you use. Style is a difficult term to define but easier to evaluate in practice. For example, all of the scenarios below result in reaching the top of the route. Which is the most meaningful ascent? Which has the most "style"?

- Della sits and watches several people do the route, then climbs it on her first try.
- Perry tries the climb every weekend all summer, taking a dozen or more falls each time. He finally succeeds in topping out, but not without resting on the rope after each move.
- Paul walks up to the base and leads the route without falling or any prior knowledge of the climb.
- Barney falls several times on his first attempt, then leaves the pro in place and climbs it without falls later that day.
- On Wilma's first attempt, she is about to fall when someone shouts up advice (which she follows) and completes the route.
- Fred walks up to the base and solos the route barefoot, without chalk, and without prior knowledge of the route (including its rating).

As you can see, if somebody says, "I climbed *Booger Slab* today," the statement can mean a lot of things. Traditionally, a no-falls, no-rests ascent was the benchmark of a valid climb (the "I climbed" part meant "I climbed without falling and without resting on the rope"). The current trend seems to be the pursuit of technical difficulty (i.e., rating number) regardless of these fine points of style, so falling, resting on the rope, previewing, and so on are accepted parts of the game for many climbers.

While these techniques are very useful when trying to improve one's climbing, it is a good idea to occasionally step back and try to see how hard you can climb in "good style"; that is, complete the route without falling and without prior knowledge of the climb. If you are leading, it is safe to say that pre-placed protection (including bolts) and slings certainly lowers the difficulty of the climb.

There is considerable vocabulary associated with style. Some climbers are starting to sound more like snowboarders or skateboarders, and promoting excessive jargon violates my prime directive.

The biggest ethical issue facing most climbers is chalk. The North Shore has a no-chalk ethic that you must read about before climbing there (page 192). Most climbers use too much chalk. Let's think about it—why do gymnasts use chalk? To get more friction while on the uneven bars? Of course not! They want to be slippery! A little chalk absorbs the sweat and oils, improving friction. When you overchalk the rock you gain nothing. Use a chalk ball, or none at all.

> Ethical climbing merely means respecting the set of rules of the climbing game that one is playing. Conversely, unethical climbing occurs when a climber attempts to use…a less restrictive set of rules.
>
> —LITO TEJADA-FLORES, *Games Climbers Play*

The author on Black Wall, *Blue Mounds.* PHOTO BY ED BURRELL

CLIMBING ETIQUETTE

Many new climbers don't realize that the noisy, rope-every-two-feet-rap-muzak atmosphere of the indoor gym conflicts with the customary outdoor climbing experience (although Taylors Falls and Devil's Lake are often so crowded that it is hard to tell the difference). Keep in mind that everyone is out here to have a positive experience, from the guided groups to families to the hard women.

Here are some suggestions to help everyone have a good time when it's crowded:

- Climbs are first come, first served. Please don't set up two feet away from another rope and get in the way. If you want a particular climb, get up earlier or show up later in the day.

- Don't drop a rope and leave it unattended. Climb and clear out for the next group.

- Allowing others to use your setup is common practice (if you are *absolutely* certain of the anchors). If you use another climber's rope, avoid protracted hangdogging and/or falling. Come back another day and do the climb with a modicum of style (or blow out your own rope).

- Never alter other peoples' anchors or setups without permission.

- If you see an unsafe situation, try to help out in a positive manner. If someone questions your setup, take the time to check it out. They may be right, or you might teach them something new.

- To avoid confusion in crowded areas, use your partner's name when you are communicating. Learn to climb with minimal communication.

- If you need to yell and scream and swear, do it at the dentist's office.

- Smoking seems to have become more common recently. A vast majority of climbers dislike the air pollution and litter; it can be a fire hazard as well. Try getting high on rocks, not proven carcinogens.

- Treat fellow climbers, park personnel, and even tourists with respect and a smile. Leave your hostilities elsewhere.

TO PARENTS AND KIDS

Kids: Have fun. If it isn't fun, convince your parents to take you to the Dells or mini-golf or Dairy Queen.

Parents: More and more kids are being brought to the crags. They are there because the parents want to climb, the kids want to climb, or the parents want the kids to climb. If Mom is climbing and Dad is belaying, who's watching the kids? Young children don't have the natural fears that keep one safe in areas of cliffs, loose rocks, water, poison ivy, and so on. Other climbers are not surrogate babysitters. If your child wants to climb, I hope you use a proper harness (including a chest harness) and helmet. If you want your kid to climb and the child doesn't, stop. Forcing a kid isn't going to make him or her tougher or stronger.

I've been a hockey parent and a soccer parent, and I've seen the best and worst of parental involvement in children's sports. Here are some recent observations that I have made of parents (mostly fathers) and children at the crags.

- A child is being belayed at Taylors Falls. The top anchor is a single sling around a block; the rope is attached by a single nonlocking carabiner. The father is standing at the bottom, unanchored, using a hip belay, and smoking a cigarette.

- Mom, Dad, baby (in car seat) and dog reach the descent gully to Cleopatra's Needle at Devil's Lake. Dad descends to a mossy slab, pack in one hand, while Mom hands down the baby. Dad, now with pack and baby, asks for the dog to be passed down. The dog, obviously the IQ champ in this family, refuses to cooperate.

- Two dads and three or four young boys are climbing at the Hawk's Nest at Devil's Lake. One boy really doesn't want to climb. His father replies with, "Get your f★@ing a★s on the rope, NOW!" After more profane verbal abuse, the child climbs while being taunted by the other boys.

- Dad puts a rope up *Jammermeister* at Taylors Falls. Kid doesn't want to climb, but starts up the loose, dangerous gully anyway. Dad continues to cajole Kid until Kid is nearly in tears. Finally Dad relents, and Kid (terrified and not trusting the rope) sort of scrapes his way down the loose crap.

There really isn't much to say about these incidents, and similar things happen in football, soccer, and every other organized sport. There is only one problem—climbing involves life and death.

Dogs. Sorry, but I have little positive to say about dogs at crowded Midwestern crags. They may be your best friend, your baby, or whatever, but they are often a nuisance to the rest of us.

Advantages of dogs	Disadvantages of dogs
Companionship to the owner	Many are noisy
Residual cuteness	Dog poop not generally cleaned up
	Walk and drool on ropes and gear
	Beg for food
	Chase wildlife

So, if you must bring dogs, 1) tie them up away from others and 2) clean up their excrement. If they bark, leave them home. If access is difficult, leave them home. Don't get defensive if people ask you to restrain your free-roaming pet.

RATINGS

The only thing certain about ratings is that there is *always* disagreement over them. Keep in mind that ratings represent an estimate of the difficulty of the climb for an average person on an average day. Body size, flexibility, balance, strength, and state of mind all play a role in determining the actual difficulty of a climb on any given day. Also keep in mind that the type of rock can influence the apparent difficulty, so ratings at an area that you are visiting for the first time often seem a bit stiff. Areas such as Devil's Lake and Blue Mounds have been historically undergraded, and the variety of rock types makes comparisons difficult. So keep in mind that 5.10 is not 5.10 is not 5.10, especially if you plan on-sight leads.

Each climbing area tends to develop its own distinct flavor of the standard rating scheme known as the Yosemite Decimal System. In this system, there are 5 classes of difficulty:

Class 1: A hiking trail.

Class 2: A scramble requiring only the occasional use of hands.

Class 3: Hands used for progress, with enough exposure that a fall may be dangerous.

Class 4: Ropes and belays used, but no intermediate protection points are used.

Class 5: The leader places intermediate pieces of protection while climbing.

Note that the term "third classing" is often used by climbers to mean solo climbing and does not necessarily mean that the route is of Class 3 difficulty. This book is concerned with fifth-class climbing, although some approach/descent routes may be described as third- or fourth-class (meaning a rope may be advisable).

This fifth class is further broken down into smaller categories (from 5.0, 5.1, 5.2 up to 5.14) to denote increasing difficulty. In the upper grades, additional suffixes (+/- or a/b/c/d) may be attached to further pinpoint the difficulty level. Thus, a 5.9- would be only slightly harder than the hardest 5.8, while a 5.11d represents the upper end of that grade. Theoretically, the rating depends only on the absolute difficulty of the hardest move on the route and not on the level of protection or type of terrain. In practice, that ideal is seldom achieved.

Aid climbs are given their original ratings. Most of these were done with pins, and clean ascents are generally not recorded here. In general, you are on your own if you wish to try clean ascents of old aid lines.

THE GEOLOGY OF MIDWESTERN ROCK CLIMBING AREAS

BY DAVID W. FARRIS AND MIKE FARRIS

Both civilization and rock climbing exist by geologic consent. Every crack, ledge, and handhold on a given cliff has a geologic basis—is it a sloper or is it a jug? Can you stand on that nubbin or will you slide off? Do cams or hexes work better? This guide covers more rock types than you might expect, so a bit of understanding about Midwestern geology is crucial for the well-traveled climber. The goal of this chapter is to tell the geologic story of various climbing areas in Minnesota and Wisconsin and to provide you with some skills to read the story yourself.

While the Earth is over 4.5 billion years old, the oldest climbable rock in these two states began its story about 1.76 billion years ago. At that time, the rocks of Devil's Lake and Blue Mounds were formed near the shore of a long-vanished sea. The next significant event transpired 700 million years later, when a rift formed in what would become Minnesota and began to split the continent apart. The rocks of Taylors Falls and The North Shore were formed at this time. The Paleozoic seas of southern Minnesota led to the sedimentary fossil-bearing rocks of Barn Bluff and Willow River. Only 12,000 years ago, glaciers scraped the land clean and created most of the topography (or, more correctly, the lack thereof) in this region. Let's look at the geological highlights of the major areas in this guide.

THE QUARTZITES OF BLUE MOUNDS AND DEVIL'S LAKE

The Sioux Quartzite at Blue Mounds State Park in Minnesota and the Baraboo Quartzite of Devil's Lake in Wisconsin share a similar origin. These rocks are the oldest climbable formations in Minnesota and Wisconsin. Approximately 1.9 to 1.8 billion years ago a mountain-building event known as the Penokean Orogeny occurred from east-central Minnesota up through northern Wisconsin and Michigan. For the next several hundred million years this mountain range was weathered away. Several quartzites, including the Sioux and the Baraboo, are thought to be a product of this erosion. About 1.76 billion years ago the banks of an ancient sea lapped against the shores of what was to become Wisconsin and Minnesota. As sand from the sea was buried, the weight of the overlying sediments compressed the former remnants of the beach into sandstone.

Both rock formations contain numerous examples of their watery origin. The most common such feature is cross bedding, which is visible as repeated inclined planes that proceed laterally across the cliff face. Cross bedding is the result of flowing water pushing around ripples and dunes. Look for ripples at the tops of the cliffs in both areas. The original thickness of the quartzites was

Caren Reich on Upper Diagonal, *Devil's Lake.* PHOTO BY DAVE REICH

thought to be over a mile; however, over time the processes of erosion reduced it to several thousand feet for the Baraboo Quartzite and far less for the Sioux Quartzite. The red and pink color of the rock is caused by the presence of small amounts of iron and manganese. Microscopic examination has revealed that the sand grains of the quartzites have been reworked several times, meaning that the grains were weathered out of pre-existing sandstones before they were incorporated into the rock we now see.

Quartzites are the metamorphic by-product of sandstones that have been deformed at high temperatures and pressures. Interestingly, the Sioux and Baraboo quartzites are of non-metamorphic origin. The quartz cement that tightly holds the rock together most likely comes from the circulation of silica-saturated ground water. Because quartzite has been fused together, it is much harder and more durable than sandstone. Therefore the rock tends to break along bedding planes; ledges and overhangs have sharp edges; and cliff faces are polished smooth. The physical properties of the rock do not lend themselves to friction climbing, as you may have discovered. Also, the wet rock is very slippery. After their formation, the rocks of Devil's Lake and Blue Mounds have separate and distinct histories.

As you will probably notice on your way to Blue Mounds, southwestern Minnesota is almost entirely flat with very few outcrops of bedrock. Glaciers are the reason for this region's billiard-table appearance. In geological terms one of the fastest and most powerful shapers of landscapes is the glacier; not much can withstand it. As a parting present to help us remember our icebound history, the glaciers left a thick and expansive coating of till. Beneath the till lies the thin but widespread Sioux Quartzite. At Blue Mounds State Park, a cliff of Sioux Quartzite rises abruptly out of the prairie. The quartzite is pink to red with the occasional yellow band. Most of the cliff faces are separated from the main body of rock. This is most easily explained as an occurrence of weathering, which most likely results from numerous instances of freeze-thaw ice wedging. On top of the cliff, evidence of glaciation can be seen in the form of highly polished whalebacks and chatter marks that trend roughly north-south. Chatter marks result when a glacier drags large boulders across the bedrock. They point in the direction of glacial movement.

The Baraboo Quartzite at Devil's Lake has a more exciting history than that of Blue Mounds. About 50 million years after the quartzite had formed, tectonic forces created a mountain range in southern Wisconsin. Tremendous forces bent and cracked the Baraboo Quartzite into a large hot-dog-bun-like structure known as a syncline. The Baraboo syncline trends west-southwest and is approximately 10 miles wide by 25 miles long. Devil's Lake lies near the south rim of the syncline. Evidence of structural deformation is visible in the quartzite. As the rock was bent, it fractured and faulted. Many of the cracks became subsequently filled with silica solution and can be seen today as white quartz-filled veins. Some of the wider fractures have been filled with angular pieces of quartzite

Bruce McDonald on Birch Flakes, *Sawmill Creek Dome.*

in addition to the quartz. Surfaces that have been offset by faulting are visible due to the presence of pearly, striated structures known as slickensides. A magnificent example of slickensides can be seen on Monster Wall.

For the next billion years the Baraboo range was weathered away, and no geologic evidence of that time period remains. About 600 million years ago, the roots of the mountain belt were exposed as islands in a Cambrian sea. The quartzite islands stood 200 to 600 feet above the water, and at their bases white-to-tan sand mixed with quartzite blocks. At this time, Wisconsin may have been within 10 degrees of the equator.

The immense gap between the East and the West Bluffs was cut by a large river at some time previous to the Pleistocene glaciers. It is not known when the river gouged through the quartzite, but evidence from drill holes indicates that the ancient river bottom was more than a thousand feet below the tops of the present bluffs. During the most recent glaciation (the Wisconsin), glaciers stopped just short of Devil's Lake. The terminal moraine from that glacier snakes its way across Wisconsin. Portions of this terminal moraine can be seen as a prominent, forest-covered ridge at the north end of Devil's Lake.

When glaciers were present, the climate in this part of Wisconsin was like that of today's Antarctic. Repeated cycles of freezing and thawing broke off numerous quartzite blocks and helped to create the talus fields we see today. Devil's Lake and most of southwest Wisconsin is located in a region known as The Driftless Area, a region that glaciers apparently missed. To the east and west the glaciers penetrated much farther south, but southwestern Wisconsin and southeastern Minnesota were spared. Evidence of this can be seen in the more mature topography and drainage basins. Heading west on Interstate 94 you can see the Mills Bluff sandstone towers, which are examples of unglaciated outcrops. Also, the Paleozoic sandstones of Petenwell Rock near Necedah are still present due to the lack of recent glaciation.

ROCKS OF THE NORTH SHORE AND NORTHERN MINNESOTA

The North Shore of Lake Superior is geologically quite complex. There are four types of rock important to climbers: basalt (Ely's Peak), rhyolite (Palisade Head, Shovel Point), anorthosite (Carlton Peak, Mystical Mountain), and diabase (Jericho Wall). First, a couple of other points of geological interest along the North Shore.

The climbing cliffs are young compared to the Ely Greenstone, which is a pillow basalt that sprang up from the ocean floor more than 2.7 billion years ago. This formation is found near Ely and is some of the oldest rock exposed anywhere. Economically more important are the vast iron ore deposits of Northern Minnesota. Primitive photosynthetic organisms caused oxygen in the world's atmosphere to slowly increase for over a billion years. By 2 billion years ago, oxygen concentrations became high enough for the dissolved iron to turn to rust and fall to the ocean floor, thereby forming most of the iron deposits worldwide.

The North Shore landscape is the result of many violent events, and the most important was the Mid-Continent (or Keweenawan) Rift. About 1.1 billion years ago, what was to become the North American continent began to split apart from Kansas to Duluth to Canada. Over a period of 20 million years, hundreds of lava flows spilled from this huge incision in the crust. If the rifting had continued, an ocean basin would have formed along the rift. For some reason the rift closed, and we therefore have a freshwater lake rather than a saltwater ocean. The thickness of all the lavas is estimated at over 8,000 meters. This mass of rock is so huge that gravity is actually stronger above it! The midcontinent gravity high is present over the length of the rift. This includes most of the climbing areas along The North Shore and Taylors Falls (what a great excuse for those days where your climbing isn't up to par).

All of the lava flows dip toward the axis of Lake Superior at approximately 10–15 degrees. However, all of the lava flows are not stacked neatly on top of one another. There are six discrete lava plateaus that are layered over each other like tilted stacks of tortillas. Different types of rocks were formed and the different rocks weathered at differing rates. Over time, this led to the rugged and beautiful coastline now present on Lake Superior.

Another fun fact: As the basalt flows cooled, many of them released gas trapped within them. Upon leaving the lava, the gas bubbles formed small holes in the tops of the flows. As fluids percolated through the rock, those empty spaces filled with layers of quartz or other minerals. As the basalts weathered away, the "fillings" were removed and today may be found on many beaches as famous Lake Superior agates.

Palisade Head and its smaller companion, Shovel Point, contain some of the best views and climbing potential along the North Shore of Lake Superior. Both are 200-foot-thick flows of red, porphyritic rhyolite, which contains an abundance of quartz, alkali feldspar, and plagioclase minerals. The rhyolite forms such spectacular cliffs because it is more resistant to weathering than the surrounding basalts.

Also included in the North Shore Volcanics is Elys Peak, which is located just south of Duluth. This locality is composed of a wedge of basalt that lies at the very base of the volcanic sequence, indicating that the rocks of Elys Peak are among the oldest of the North Shore lavas.

THE ANORTHOSITES OF CARLTON PEAK AND THE LAKE COUNTY ROAD 6 AREAS

Carlton Peak rises to a height of 924 feet above Lake Superior, providing visitors a spectacular view of the surrounding area. In the fall this vista is especially rewarding due to the red and gold colors of the maple, birch, and aspen. As one looks to the southwest and northeast along the shore of the lake various other knobs can be seen protruding upward. One may ask, "Why are these high points here?" Carlton Peak and these other knobs are composed almost entirely of the rock anorthosite. Anorthosite is much more resistant to weathering than the surrounding rock known as diabase. Consequently, more of the anorthosite is left behind after a given amount of time, and a significant topographic feature (a hill) is created.

The anorthosites along Lake Superior formed as part of a large intrusive body of magma known as the Duluth Complex. The Duluth Complex formed approximately 1.1 billion years ago and is associated with the mid-continental rifting event that occurred at that time. Over the years, many people have studied the Duluth Complex because of its unusual suite of rock types and potentially economically important resources. Traces of platinum, copper, nickel, and titanium have been found. The Duluth Complex is over 150 miles long and stretches from Duluth to Grand Portage. It is oldest at Grand Portage and Duluth and youngest in the middle near Tofte. The anorthosite domes were formed when plagioclase crystals were separated at depth and the resulting crystal mush was injected upward, segregating it from its magmatic body of origin. In other words, chunks of rock were burped up from far below the surface.

Along the North Shore of Lake Superior, anorthosite is relatively common. However, elsewhere in the world the rock type is rare, so the anorthosites of north-eastern Minnesota have been heavily studied. Other localities where anorthosite is found include New York, Labrador, and Norway. Anorthosite is composed almost entirely of the plagioclase mineral labradorite. Some specimens of labradorite shimmer with iridescence when illuminated correctly. On fresh surfaces, the rock is light green and has a tendency to be sharp due to its glass-like fracture patterns. It's hard to believe, but erosion has made the rock smoother than it might be otherwise! Individual crystals can be up to several inches in length, and, due to its large grain size, we know the rock cooled slowly.

THE BASALTS OF INTERSTATE STATE PARK (TAYLORS FALLS)

Taylors Falls, also known as Interstate State Park, has a geologic history that spans an immense amount of time. Events shaping the landscape we now see have occurred from about 1.1 billion years ago to a few thousand years ago.

The main body of rock at Taylors Falls is composed of a black-to-gray, fine-grained igneous rock known as basalt. Basalt is composed mainly of minerals rich in iron, magnesium, and calcium. It forms when magma of the appropriate chemical composition is spewed onto the surface of the Earth, causing it to cool rapidly. Individual crystals become larger when they dissipate heat over a longer period of time. Therefore, when an igneous rock is fine-grained, one knows that it cooled quickly.

About 1.1 billion years ago, the basalt we now see was poured onto the Earth's surface as one of a number of large basalt flows that extend northward

David Dahl on Witch's Tit, *Taylors Falls.*

into Wisconsin and Minnesota as part of a greater system of volcanic activity known as the Midcontinental Rift. Interstate Park contains the southernmost exposed flows. The sequence is over 20,000 feet thick; remember the midcontinent gravity high discussed earlier.

At Taylors Falls there are ten smaller basalt flows. The top of each flow is marked by a "bubbly layer," whereas the base of each is more massive. These "bubbles" or vesicles are small round holes in the surface of the rock and are formed when bubbles of gas escape while the lava is cooling. The gas moves upward, and therefore vesicles are always found on the top of a flow. Often the vesicles are filled with secondary minerals such as quartz, chlorite or zeolites. In places, the rock has a somewhat greenish hue, which is due to slight metamorphism. When an igneous rock cools, it contracts. If the rock cools quickly it will fracture and form joint sets perpendicular to the cooling surface. These joint sets define many of the rock formations and climbs at Taylors Falls.

After the basalt was formed 1.1 billion years ago, there is a 600-million-year gap in the geologic record. Five hundred million years ago, an inland sea began to cover the basalt flows and form sandstone. Above the cliffs at Taylors Falls, an unusual rock formation known as the Millstreet Conglomerate is found. Chunks of basalt as big as microwave ovens are supported by a matrix of sand. Small gastropods and trilobites are found within the conglomerate. Careful identification of those fossils led to the above date for the sandstone. The Millstreet Conglomerate formed when the Cambrian sea moved over rocky beaches composed of the basalt. As sedimentation continued, the conglomerate gave way to sandstone (as the underlying basalt was buried), and that procession can be seen today simply by hiking up the bluffs surrounding the St. Croix River.

The uppermost stratigraphic unit at Interstate Park is composed of glacial till, which is unsorted and contains many different rock types of all different sizes. The composition of till depends on whatever the glacier had previously run over and was carrying along. During the Quaternary Period (2 million years ago to the present) Minnesota was glaciated multiple times. At present, we are in the midst of a warm interglacial period. The last glaciers began to retreat approximately 12 to 13 thousand years ago. The melting glacier formed Glacial Lake Duluth, a larger version of today's Lake Superior. That lake drained through the valley of the present-day St. Croix River, causing the volume of water in the river to be much greater than what we see today. That earlier version of the St. Croix River cut deeply into the basalt flows, forming the cliffs that today attract so many climbers.

Interstate Park claims to have the "world's largest potholes," and those were also made possible by the increased water volume in the river. The potholes were formed as gravel and other grindstones were caught in eddies or irregularities in the basalt. Once an initial hole was excavated by the water, ever bigger grindstones could be trapped, which continually accelerated the excavation process. In the Interstate Park interpretative center there are grindstones as round and as big as bowling balls. The potholes grew up to tens of feet in diameter and can be 50–60 feet deep. The interiors of the potholes are polished smooth, and some of the more slippery climbs are found within them.

THE SEDIMENTARY ROCKS OF RED WING (BARN BLUFF)

Barn Bluff, located in Red Wing, is a product of ancient seas. The horizontal sediments that make up the bluff were laid down beginning over 500 million years ago. Rocks of the bluff record the movements of that long-vanished sea until about 450 million years ago.

Barn Bluff contains four distinct units from those ancient Paleozoic seas. The four units are (oldest to youngest): the Franconia greensand, the St. Lawrence siltstone, the Jordan sandstone, and the Oneida dolomite. Contained within each rock unit is a record of a changing world. The seas went in, and the seas went out. Greensands indicate shallow water which was low in oxygen. Within the siltstone, fossils of long extinct animals such as trilobites and marine arthropods can be found if you look hard enough. The sandstones are remnants of a beach or near-shore environment. Dolomites indicate a deep, quiet sea. Modern day carbonates (limestones and dolomites) form in locations like the Bahamas. So if you were hoping for a tropical island paradise, you're in the right place, just a little late.

After the Ordovician Period there is a tremendous gap in the geologic record at Barn Bluff. The next 450 million years of time and rock are simply not present. However, there is evidence that something did happen to the rocks during that period. The west side of the bluff is cut by a steeply dipping fault. Rocks on that side of the bluff are roughly 150 feet higher than rocks to the east. A vertical zone of crushed rock that extends all the way up the bluff denotes the fault plane. Some time before the Cretaceous Period a gradual up-arching of the sediments between Red Wing and Rochester took place. In other parts of the world, similar structures have proved to be good traps for oil. In this instance, however, all that has been trapped is water.

Andrzej Malewicz on Living All over Me, *Barn Bluff.*

You may wonder why Barn Bluff sits out on its own, isolated from the main banks of the Mississippi. The bluff's oblong, torpedo-like shape suggests its origin. It was an island in the raging torrent of the post-glacial Mississippi. Also of glacial origin is the 65-foot-thick layer of drift that sits atop the Paleozoic sediments. The glacial drift is composed of sand, gravel, and windblown silt known as loess.

Bruce McDonald on Balcony Center, *Blue Mounds.*

BLUE MOUNDS

> There I lay staring upward, while the stars wheeled over. . . . Faint to
> my ears came the gathered rumour of all lands: the springing and the
> dying, the song and the weeping, and the slow, everlasting groan of
> overburdened stone.
>
> —J.R.R. TOLKIEN

The rocks of Blue Mounds State Park rise almost apologetically from the surrounding plains. On their slow voyage west, early European settlers noted a bluish tint to the rocks when the sun was low in the sky. These are the same people who lived in sod houses made of prairie grasses and clay, survived massive storms without weather radar, and collected bushels of grasshoppers for cash bounties.

Native Americans had discovered Blue Mounds and nearby Pipestone National Monument far earlier. At Pipestone National Monument, the hard quartzite was quarried away to reveal the thin layers of soft pipestone (Catlinite). This pipestone hardens when exposed to air, but is still carvable. The rock was used by Native Americans to produce pipes and other carvings, and the pipestone was traded far and wide. The side trip to Pipestone National Monument is worthwhile, as is the jaunt to the Jeffers Petroglyphs northeast of Luverne. There is no climbing at either location.

The other way in which Native Americans may have used the rocks was as a natural buffalo trap. Bison may have been stampeded over the tops of the cliffs, but there is no evidence that this actually happened at Blue Mounds. At the south end of the cliffs there is a 1,250-foot line of rocks that aligns with the sun on the first day of spring and fall. This may have been constructed by Europeans, Native Americans, or bored space aliens—nobody really knows.

The rock is quartzite—not the soft, porous sandstone of the Driftless Area, but the same hard, impeccable quartzite found at Devil's Lake, Wisconsin. The result is the opportunity for steep face climbing, some big roofs, and more moderate face, crack, and chimney climbs than anywhere else in Minnesota or Wisconsin.

Emergency contact: Call the Rock County Sheriff at 911, or call the park office (507-283-1307). The public phone nearest the north parking area is at the park office; from the south parking area go to the Interpretive Center if the gates are open, or go into Luverne. The nearest hospital is five blocks east of U.S. Highway 75 on Luverne Street in Luverne. Report all accidents to the park office.

BLUE MOUNDS OVERVIEW

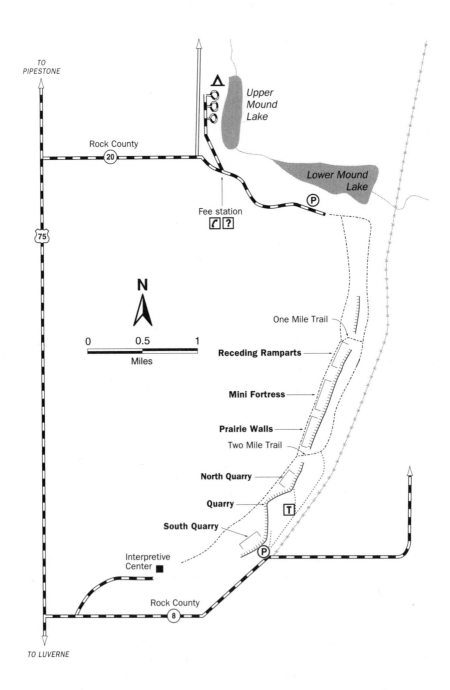

TO
PIPESTONE

Rock County
20

75

Upper
Mound
Lake

Lower Mound
Lake

Fee station

N

0   0.5   1
Miles

One Mile Trail

Receding Ramparts

Mini Fortress

Prairie Walls

Two Mile Trail

North Quarry

Quarry

South Quarry

Interpretive
Center

T

P

Rock County
8

TO LUVERNE

The climbing environment: By far the best time of the year to visit Blue Mounds is in the spring. The southwest corner of the state is often the first to thaw, and temperatures at the base of the climbs can be 20–30° warmer than the predicted highs in the Twin Cities. This also means, of course, that temperatures can be brutally hot in mid-summer. Autumn can be as pleasant as spring if you aren't too tired of traveling by that time of the year.

While the rock is very much like Devil's Lake quartzite, it does climb a bit differently. The harder climbs tend to outwit roofs, and there are few steep routes on small horizontal edges. The other difference you'll notice is the relative lack of people. You can always climb at Blue Mounds by yourself. Most traffic goes to the major walls, and many unexplored climbs wait to be done. Be sure to send me the details for the next edition of this guide.

There is a lot of poison ivy scattered around these cliffs, mainly at the base and in the approach gullies. Most of us are familiar with the three-part leaves of the growing plant, but in the leafless spring look for the remnants of woody stems with white berries. Prickly pear cactus is also common, especially on top. Cactus spines can take months to work themselves out of your fingertips (I've done research on this personally). When you are walking around on the tops of the climbs, try to walk on bare rock to avoid trampling the vegetation and to avoid impaling yourself.

There are several rare plant species associated with this rock formation. In the spring, temporary pools form in shallow depressions in the rock and support a number of species that are found nowhere else in Minnesota. If you encounter a muddy basin in the rock, avoid walking through it for this reason. In addition, a rare species of prickly pear cactus (along with a similar, but common species) also inhabits the cracks of Blue Mounds.

Leading is possible on the obvious crack climbs, but in general the harder routes can only be protected with some trickery and very small nuts, or not at all. Cams are not as useful as hexes because of the angular nature of the cracks and very low friction of the rock. There is absolutely no fixed protection here, and none may be placed. Setting up top-ropes can be an adventure, as many of the routes are found on semi-detached sections of the cliff. Look around for an easy approach before jumping! I've included approach info for most buttress tops.

I have used the original pamphlet by the Zumbro River Alpine Club (ZRAC) and North Shore Climbers Group (NSCG), Scott Wurdinger's *A Rock Climbing Guidebook to Blue Mounds State Park* (1989), and *Prairie Walls* (1989) by Hynek and Landmann (Granite Publishing, Madison, WI) as resources. The latter guide should still be available. Routes not previously reported but probably climbed were assigned names. First ascent data is sketchy; hopefully, the few claimed first ascents will stimulate you to send in corrections or other new routes.

Immediately after I reorganized the previous guide to reflect the lack of parking on the south end, parking was again permitted there. There is now an eight-space parking area on the south end of The Mound. Do not park along the road, as you will be ticketed. Try to conserve space in this lot by carpooling as much as possible or by walking in from the north end. The lot won't be getting bigger, so help your fellow climbers out by leaving as much space as possible.

The Minnesota Climbing Management Plan: *Climber Registration*—Rock climbing permits will be valid for the calendar year and may be obtained free of charge, in person or by mail, by contacting the park office.

Closures—Rock climbing is generally permitted on all natural rock faces within Blue Mounds State Park. Climbers should be aware that rock integrity varies throughout the park.

Alteration of the Natural Environment—The local climbing ethic at Blue Mounds State Park discourages the use of white chalk. Climbers are strongly encouraged to use chalk that blends with the color of the rock, or a clear chalk substitute. Any visible residue should be removed by the climber.

Services: The town of Luverne has all major services. As you drive around, look at the buildings made of Sioux quartzite from the quarry in the park. The freeway fast food strip has pretty much killed the downtown eateries. The Magnolia Steak House (just south of Interstate 90) and Scottie's (just north of I–90) offer different ways to experience the local culture.

The park itself contains a small, charming campground. It is often busy on weekends, and reservations are recommended. The water in the campground is high in nitrates; BYOB if you are sensitive to excessive agricultural runoff. If the water is off in the campground, check at the walk-in campground between sites 1 and 2. The water will be left on at that location as long as possible each fall. Other camping options are limited.

Approach: The cliffs are located about 5 miles north of Luverne in Blue Mounds State Park. Virtually all climbers approach the park from Interstate 90. Proceed north on U.S. Highway 75 into the bustling hamlet of Luverne. From the stoplight at the intersection of US 75 and Main Street, continue 4.4 miles north and turn east on Rock County 20 to reach the main park entrance (for registration, camping, etc.). To reach the south parking lot, turn east on Rock County 8, which is 2.4 miles north of Main Street. Proceed less than two miles to a small parking lot on the left. Please carpool or otherwise limit the number of vehicles per group in this lot.

The cliff faces generally east, and the routes are described from south to north (left to right from the base). The rock is naturally divided into a series of buttresses 20–100 feet wide. Access to the top is available by scrambling up gullies between the buttresses. Unless otherwise noted, the climbs are found on the east face of each buttress. Most of the buttresses are relatively easy to spot from below. The climbs in this guide are found in five distinct areas: the South

Quarry Area, the North Quarry Area, the Prairie Walls Area, the Mini Fortress Area, and the Receeding Ramparts Area. The quarry itself is loose and dangerous and is avoided by sensible climbers.

From the south parking lot, walk north through the grass, generally along a fence to your right. The South Quarry Area is reached by branching left almost immediately, following signs to the quarry. The North Quarry Area is reached by taking a possibly inobvious trail just past the outhouse and cottonwood a few minutes up the fenceline. The Prairie Walls Area is obvious from the fenceline after a ten-minute walk. The Mini Fortress Area and the southern buttresses on the Receeding Ramparts are best reached from the Prairie Walls Area, while the northern end is reached by continuing along the fenceline.

These northern areas might be more quickly reached from the beach parking area at Lower Mound Lake. Proceed past the entrance station (after paying fees) and drive to the beach. Walk down the service road to the spillway at the east end of the lake and take the mowed trail south. Pass some short cliffs which quickly degenerate. After about ten minutes, the One-Mile Trail comes down from above (possibly unmarked, but mowed). The first climbable cliffs you encounter are a few minutes past this.

SOUTH QUARRY AREA

This is the closest area to the south parking lot and can be reached in a few minutes. There are not many classic routes here, but they can serve as the equivalent of fast food—quick and filling (if not satisfying).

From the parking lot, take the first trail to your left, which heads toward the quarry. You will meet the rock at the base of Quarry Corner Buttress. To reach the other buttresses, work up and left along the cliff line for about 20 meters, then turn right and pass between two boulders. Walk between the cliff band and Sun Drop II Tower; Wasp Haven Buttress is on the right. Descend through some small boulders to Red Rock Buttress.

RED ROCK BUTTRESS

Access the top using the chimney on the left side of the buttress.

1. **Coyote Blues** (5.9+) ★ Start just around the corner from *Off Width* on the south face. Bounce up a couple of moves, over the overhang, then move up and left to a more moderate finish.
2. **Off Width** (5.7) ★ An apparently easy crack becomes puzzling above the horizontal ledge.
3. **Deception Ledge** (5.9) ★★ A tricky face above the horizontal ledge.
4. **Six Footer** (5.8) ★ A long reach will stymie the vertically challenged.

RED ROCK BUTTRESS

WASP HAVEN BUTTRESS—RIGHT

WASP HAVEN BUTTRESS

Access to the left or right. Several opportunities for short but harder routes exist to the right of the routes listed here.

5. **Inside Corner** (5.4) ★ On the south face there is a right-facing corner.

6. **EZ Chimney** (5.4) ★ The chimney in the middle.

SUN DROP II TOWER

This tower presents a couple of short, easy lead options. Small hexes or medium stoppers for top anchors.

7. **Junior Varsity** (5.10a) ★ The northwest arete, nearest the main cliff. Start up the arete on large holds, then lurch right over a bulge. Varsity climbers should try the direct west face (harder) or south face (even harder); they have no recorded ascents. FA: M. Farris, 1999.

8. **Burnt-Out Candle** (5.5) ★ As you approach this tower from the parking lot, note that the north face is broken by ledges and cracks. This route climbs the right-facing corner leading to ledges and more cracks. FA: Eric Landmann and Don Hynek, 1988.

9. **Piece o' Cake** (5.6) ★ Just left of the previous route is a splitter crack leading to a ledge. FA: Eric Landmann and Don Hynek, 1988.

10. **Esterify Me Again!** (5.6) A goofy-looking crack on the east face. FA: Eric Landmann and Don Hynek, 1988.

HIDDEN BUTTRESS

Directly south of Quarry Corner Buttress. Access is to the left.

11. **Park Bench** (5.7) ★ A chimney with an overhang partway up marks the left edge of the south face. Take the chimney and face just to the right.

12. **Elm Tree Pinch** (5.7) ★ Up the dihedral on the outside corner, then keep following corners to the top.

13. **Thin Line** (5.7) ★★ Start beneath a corner above the overhangs high on the face. Work up the face and cut left into a shallow corner. The bottom may hold moves tougher than the rating suggests, or maybe my hands were too cold that day.

14. **Hidden Direct** (5.9) ★★ Forge boldly over the roof and up the corner rather than chickening out as on *Thin Line*.

15. **Handicapp** (5.9) ★★ Wear your flat 'at for this one. Climb up flakes under right side of overhang. Make a delicate traverse right around roof, then up. Don't use the wall behind you.

SUN DROP II TOWER—NORTH

HIDDEN AND QUARRY CORNER BUTTRESSES

QUARRY CORNER BUTTRESS

The quarry trail meets the cliffline here. Access to the left. There are possible routes to the right of *Acute Corner*; potential residual loose rock from blasting prevents me from listing any.

16. **The Corner** (5.5) ★ Chimney up a few feet to a corner on the arete. Follow corners to the top.

17. **Headbanger** (5.7) A spooky, wide crack/chimney with lots of loose junk. If you insist on climbing it, keep your belayer and others well uphill out of the fall line.

18. **Acute Corner** (5.10c/d) ★★ Start on the very prow under the roof. Muscle up to the triangular roof, then make a move or two in the black crack on the left. A gym climber's delight.

THE QUARRY

Climbing here is not a good idea. There is lots of loose stuff, some of which is bigger than daddy's Volvo. With a mile of decent rock, and hundreds of new routes to put up, why are you even thinking about climbing here?

THE NORTH QUARRY AREA

This area contains a good selection of hard face, crack, and roof problems, with a few nice moderate routes sprinkled in for good measure. On hot days, the trees provide comforting shade for belayers and spectators. The best approach is to hike along the fenceline from the south. Near the lone cottonwood and outhouse, a trail angles up and left to the base of Kanaranzi Buttress.

Hiking south of Kanaranzi Buttress, go down a few feet and around a large boulder. After a few more feet you come to a prominent buttress with a large roof on its east face. This is Big Roof Buttress and is home to *Death Scream*. About 100 feet farther south is a buttress with a similar but smaller roof, and a number of large talus blocks at its base. This is Two Boulders Buttress. Continue south a few yards to reach ORC Wall.

ORC WALL

Time to explore. Two outcrops south of Two Boulders Buttress and north of the quarry is this small rock.

19. **First Blood** (5.6) Over two chockstones in a "big hollow crack" on the left side.

20. **Lumberjack Crack** (5.5) A crack angling up and right.

TWO BOULDERS BUTTRESS

21. **Dirty Dawg** (5.8) ★ A decent route; it appears to have cleaned up its act. On the right edge of the south face is a shallow, right-facing corner. Paw your way up this, or go up the left side of the outside corner (*Dirty Dawg Direct*, 5.9).

22. **Mad Dawg** (5.9) ★ 20/20 vision will help you spot the handholds to make this route go. Take a direct line up the left corner of the east face of Two Boulders Buttress, right of *Dirty Dawg Direct*.

TWO BOULDERS BUTTRESS

AGONY BUTTRESS

AGONY BUTTRESS

23. **Death Scream** (5.10c/d) ★★ This imposing roof requires "enthusiasm et lucidité," to quote Rebuffat. Go up the crack leading to the right edge of the main roof, try to rest, then swing out left and pull the roof. If this is too tame, do a harder variation to the left.

KANARANZI BUTTRESS

This buttress, one of the taller ones in the park, has something for almost every-one. The routes are found on both the south and east faces. The best approach to the top from Kanaranzi Buttress is a Class 3 chimney a few yards south of *Triple Chockstone*. To reach the edge of the cliff, look for a convenient chockstone near the south end of the buttress. The south face has three large dihedrals, while the east face is characterized by a band of roofs near the top.

SOUTH FACE

24. **Triple Chockstone** (5.5) The name pretty much says it all. The leftmost of the three chimneys.

25. **5/8** (5.9) ★ Inflation, I guess. Take the east face to the left of the middle chimney, just right of a triangular overhang. Climb up flakes and skirt the overhang at the top to the left.

26. **The Squeeze** (5.7) ★ The middle chimney is best climbed by avoiding chim-ney techniques as much as possible.

27. **The Layback** (5.11b/c) ★★★ I can never figure out how to attempt the crux. Left of the rightmost chimney is a large roof about 12' up. Plod up the flake/crack, whimpering as you go.

28. **K-1** (5.9+) ★★ If *K-1* is in Minnesota, why is K2 in Pakistan? On the right margin of the right-hand chimney (the one with a huge block at its top) is a flake. When the flake ends, improvise straight up, staying on the right side of the chimney.

29. **Kanaranzi Left** (5.11a) ★★ Just left of the next route is a very thin black crack. Proceed straight up until you're about even with the roof, about 66.7% of the way up, then bail up and right.

30. **Kanaranzi Corner** (5.7) ★★ The roofs and arete add more exposure than you usually find here. There is a dihedral at the junction of the south and east faces. Climb the corner up to the first roof, go right, then up the east-facing crack to the upper roof (which can easily be made harder, but hardly made easier).

KANARANZI BUTTRESS—
SOUTH FACE

EAST FACE

31. **Crazy Crack** (5.7) ★★ Often led, it tops out at a slight notch at the top left side of the *Purgatory* wall. Start in a crack about 5' right of the notch and go up, zig left, and end at the notch.

32. **Stairway to Heaven** (5.11) ★ Start about 6' right of *Crazy Crack* and keep that distance until you are squeezed left by the big roof at the top. You could go over the roof (5.11b). Contrived at the top.

33. **Purgatory** (5.11a) ★★★ Maybe the classic hard route at Blue Mounds. It starts in a little square black niche about 15 feet right of *Crazy Crack*. Work upward, possibly moving left to take advantage of vertical cracks/flakes. Three roofs at the top may represent eternal damnation for some.

34. **Stairway to Hell** (5.11) ★★ If the previous two routes leave you with some extra energy, start about 6' right of *Purgatory* and go straight up. Expect horizontal ledges and a thin, hairline crack which forms the line but provides few holds.

35. **The Crack** (5.7) ★★ A chimney, an overhanging jamcrack, and a bit of a stem provide an entertaining view of harder climbs on both sides.

36. **Kanaranzi Right** (5.9+) ★★★ Excellent, varied climbing that continually makes you think. If you miss the secret handhold, it is 5.10. Start just left of some talus boulders on redder rock with large holds. Work up and right to white rock, cut to the left side of the large overhang and pull it. Scamper to the top.

KANARANZI BUTTRESS—
EAST FACE

37. **The Guillotine** (5.9) ★★ Just around the corner from *Kanaranzi Right* is a north-facing climb that is a cut above many routes here. Start up the crack.

LITTLE RANZI BUTTRESS

A few feet north of Kanaranzi Buttress. The best approach is up to the clifftop via the Kanaranzi Buttress approach.

38. **Little Ranzi Crack** (5.7+) ★ Climb up the shallow indentation in the center of the face. A tricky start and a balance move at the top shatter any delusions of the former 5.6 rating.

39. **Round Off** (5.10c) Stay off. Start on the north face, just right of the arete, climb up a few feet, cut left to the east face, then to the top.

FLATTOP BUTTRESS

Flattop Buttress is characterized by a huge block in the chimney to its left and a big red roof about 15 feet up.

40. **Cactus Jam** (5.10b) ★★ On the south side of the rock there is a thin crack about 4' left of a black streak above the roof. Starting from a vertical fin of rock, climb up to this crack.

41. **Dave's Dangle** (5.11a) ★★ Just to the right of the prow, this strenuous route goes over the roof to a thin crack right of some red rock. Start just right of the large boulder and look for a crucial block under the roof (if you can see it underneath all the chalk).

42. **Diagonal Crack** (5.6) ★ On the east face, a crack leads to a hanging corner and to a roof. Large gear if you lead it.

TYRANNOSAURUS

No reported routes, but the photo should stimulate some of you. A few yards north of Flattop Buttress.

BISON BUTTRESS

Just north of the Tyrannosaurus is another detached block, this one with an inset on the east face and a prominent crack running through an overhang on the right. Approach from the left (Class 3 ledges on the back) or the right (up the chimney and jump the gap—probably easier).

43. **Celtis Crack** (5.6) ★ A wall leads to a large ledge (the inset). Climb the left-hand crack, trying not to be too indecisive. FA: Kathy Shea and Mike Farris, 1999.

44. **Destination Unknown** (5.10) ★★ A few feet left of *Oath of Fealty* is a line of flakes leading up the steep wall.

FLATTOP BUTTRESS

TYRANNOSAURUS

45. **Oath of Fealty** (5.10b) ★★★ This crack is about 40 feet tall and overhangs 8'. A surprising and unusual route for this area in that it's actually easier than it looks. Take a #4 Camalot or two if you lead it.

PRAIRIE WALLS AREA

A great place to get that spring sunburn. The southeast-facing rock shelters climbers from the wind and reflects heat onto the winter-bleached April skin of many climbers. From the parking area, hike along the trail, parallel to the fence, for about 20 minutes until you encounter a long stretch of clean cliffs. These are the Prairie Walls.

The best summit access from the left end of this area is the marked trail, which attains the top a few yards south of Yellow Lichen Buttress. On the right end, there is a large chimney between Everyday and Chimney Buttresses that can be scrambled to the top. Intervening gullies can be passed with various degrees of difficulty as noted below. Watch for poison ivy throughout this area.

TREE LEDGE BUTTRESS

Just right of the marked trail.

46. **Berry Brothers** (5.6) Tree Ledge, *Berry Brothers* . . . have fun on this botanical adventure. Start below a squat, flat-topped boulder just right of the trail leading to the top.

BOKE'S BUTTRESS

A short buttress left of Yellow Lichen Buttress.

47. **Last Grasp** (5.7) ★ A previous guide sayeth, "Climb up to the third ledge on the left side of the buttress," then step right to the nose.

48. **Last Day's Misery** (5.6) ★ Up the middle of the face toward a small depression at the top.

YELLOW LICHEN BUTTRESS

The south wall is the namesake of Yellow Lichen Buttress and has a really nice climb on it. It might be easiest to use the marked trail to reach the top.

49. **Yellow Lichen Crack** (5.9) ★★ The south wall has a short but trying intermittent crack.

50. **Paul's A-Version** (5.5) Cut left to a left-facing corner after climbing 10' of the next route.

51. **Pedestal Left** (5.4) ★★ A nice crack with good stemming for the beginner. Climb the dihedral to the left of the obvious nose or pedestal.

52. **Pedestal Right** (5.5) ★★ A slightly more difficult route than its counterpart to the left. From the ledge you may climb left and up the face of the pedestal (5.8+).

53. **Cactus Platform Face** (5.7) ★ From the ledge, forge right to the upper right corner of the face.

**YELLOW LICHEN BUTTRESS AND
BOTTOM BOULDERS BUTTRESS**

Bruce McDonald on Yellow Lichen Crack, *Yellow Lichen Buttress.*

54. **Behind the Trees** (5.6) ★ A couple of trees flank a nose of rock. Climb the nose to a corner.

BOTTOM BOULDERS BUTTRESS

Just right of Yellow Lichen Buttress.

55. **Layback Crack** (5.7) ★ Find a reddish, triangular overhang near the bottom of the left side. Start up the large flake to the left of that overhang, up to the top of a block, and keep going up the corner.

56. **Bulge Across** (5.8) ★ Angle right from the top of the block.

57. **Piernas Borraches** (5.10) ★★ Up the red triangular overhang to the thin crack above. FA: Eric Landmann and Don Hynek, 1988.

58. **Save-Me-Tree** (5.8) ★ The tree is pretty much gone. Find a crack on the right side of Bottom Boulders Buttress with a twig partway up.

MANY CRACKS BUTTRESS

Just left of Saturday Buttress, it is best left as an offering to the lichen gods. There's much better climbing on either side of this buttress.

59. **Third Time's a Charm** (5.8) Dirty and hardly worth doing. Up the pedestal, trend left.

60. **Cussin' Crack** (5.8+) Dirty and hardly worth doing. Up the pedestal, trend right.

61. **Noseprick** (5.8) Dirty and hardly worth doing. The next crack right.

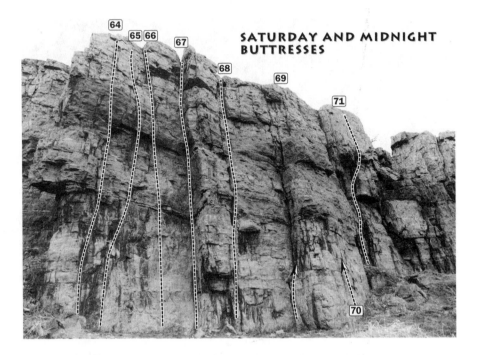

SATURDAY AND MIDNIGHT BUTTRESSES

62. **The Klinger** (5.9) Dirty and hardly worth doing. The next crack right.

63. **Incapacitation** (5.8) Dirty and hardly worth doing. The next crack right.

SATURDAY BUTTRESS

Saturday Buttress has a major left-facing corner in its middle (*Jasper's Dihe-dral*). This is one of the most popular destinations in the park. The rock seems slightly more broken and loose than normal, so be forewarned. The chimney behind the buttress has some future bowling balls, too.

64. **Black and Blue Bulge** (5.8+) ★★ There are three routes to the left of *Jasper's Dihedral*. Find a short, thin seam at ground level about 13' left of the corner. Start a few inches left of this seam and climb up to a short finger crack. From the left end of the overhang, power up a red bulge on perfect Devil's Lake–style edges. This will be easier if overchalked and harder if you climb the thin crack to the left.

65. **Black Wall** (5.9) ★★ Start in the seam mentioned above or to the right (harder). Stay about 6' right of *Black and Blue Bulge*. Clear the overhang to the left of two black streaks (crux).

66. **Gulliver's Travels** (5.7+) ★★ Start 6' left of *Jasper's Dihedral* and climb directly up to a short corner at the top of the wall.

67. **Jasper's Dihedral** (5.8) ★★★ This excellent route is often led (large hexes/cams), but be prepared for some fun near the top. Climb the large left-facing corner.

68. **Ivy Right** (5.5) ★★ You're gonna need an ocean. . . . Just right of the top of *Jasper's Dihedral* is a small notch. Climb the crack leading to it. A nice lead.

69. **Old Stump** (5.7) ★ Follow a smaller, left-facing corner with a shrub on the right side of the buttress.

70. **Alexandra David Neal** (5.8) ★ Slide up the face and corner about 6' right of *Old Stump*.

MIDNIGHT BUTTRESS
Use the chimney behind Saturday Buttress to reach the top.

71. **Mean Streak** (5.10a) ★★★ Zip up the chimney and traverse right under an overhang. The fun begins after you pull over the roof. A cool route.

72. **Easy Street** (5.6) ★ Climb the broken corner to the left of *Prow-ess* and zip up to a platform and a south-facing crack. The relationship between this route and another called *The Obvious Crack* (5.7) listed in the *Prairie Walls* guide is not obvious at all; see that book for a description.

73. **Prow-ess** (5.10c) ★ Easier after you've done it once. Climb dark rock just left of *Midnight Chimney*. Take the overhang on a thin bracket to the left, then move right and try to grab the correct hold. A 5.9 version supposedly exists up the left side of the face, but darned if we could find it.

74. **Midnight Chimney** (5.4) Another 5.4 chimney that nobody climbs.

MIDNIGHT AND SUNDAY BUTTRESSES

SUNDAY AND EVERYDAY BUTTRESSES

SUNDAY BUTTRESS

If you only have a few hours to climb, come here; you'll blow yourself out with time to spare. The large balcony or window is the easiest landmark to spot. Clamber across boulders and make an exposed step around the southeast corner of the buttress (Class 3) to set up.

75. **No Go Crack** (5.12b) ★★ If you flash this on-sight, have your friends buy you dinner at the Magnolia Steak House. A black face leads to an overhanging thin crack below the left side of the balcony. Exit the balcony at its left edge as well. It has been led.

76. **Balcony Center** (5.10a) ★★★ Start up the crack and face to its left. Grab the jugs, levitate up to the balcony, and try to climb over the center of the balcony roof. Lots of fun for those with simian tendencies.

77. **Balcony Right** (5.9+) ★★★ Start just right of the crack and pass through the right side of the balcony. Leadable, but not appropriate for 5.9 leaders.

78. **Cactus Capers** (5.10b/c) ★★★ The large protruding block on top is directly above a jog in the main roof about halfway up. Smooth, difficult to rest, a reachy crux—just another route at Blue Mounds.

79. **Unknown** (5.?) Climb within a few feet of the right edge of the buttress and subdue the overhang at a thin crack. There is no evidence that this has actually been done.

80. **Everyday Chimney** (5.4) ★ Guess what?

EVERYDAY BUTTRESS

This is the buttress that begins just left of the access chimney and contains four steep and popular routes. Getting to the top is not easy. Gain the top of Sunday Buttress and walk to the far north end. A sloping foothold on the very corner of the buttress allows a step across to Everyday Buttress. This is a textbook example of alpine third class. Please do not climb in the isolated grotto behind this buttress as the vegetation is too delicate to withstand trampling.

81. **Jammer** (5.9) ★★★ Good advice. Near the left edge of the buttress is a black crack and corner system leading to a vexing little roof about two-thirds of the way up. Often led, often unsuccessfully.

82. **Lechery** (5.10b) ★★★ Home of one of the world's sharpest fingerlocks. About 8' right of *Jammer* is an overhang halfway up with a right-facing corner below. Climb to the corner and thrust right and into the upper crack.

83. **Treachery** (5.9+) ★★★ You will be betrayed by a lack of footwork. On the right side of the buttress is a left-facing corner that matches the right-facing corner on *Lechery*. Climb directly up to this and on to the top.

84. **Debauchery** (5.8) ★★★ This fine route was accidentally left out of my previous book. Just left of the access chimney is a shallow corner on the north face of the buttress. Follow these corners to the top.

CHIMNEY BUTTRESS

This is just right of the chimney that provides access to the top and has some shrubs and trees at the base. Watch for poison ivy in the chimney. Routes are possible in the access chimney, but are best left for non-busy weekends.

CHIMNEY BUTTRESS—LEFT

85. **Jugs of Whine** (5.9) ★ Start just right of the chimney and improvise up a shallow corner. Skirt the upper overhang either left or right (harder), depending on your setup. Don't use the blocks at the base of the chimney.

86. **Roofs** (5.9+) ★★ Climb directly up to the overhang and left-facing corner about 15' right of the buttress corner.

87. **Poika** (5.11a) ★★ Climb directly up to the roof and forge through. Very sequential. *Poika* is Swedish for "little boy." FA: Kristoffer Johnson.

88. **X** (5.7) ★★ The choice of a new generation. The large roof system on *Roofs* ends about 30' to the right. *X* ascends the crack at the right-hand edge of the roof to a right-facing corner. Leadable.

89. **Y** (5.8+) ★ Why not? Climb straight up, 6' right of X. The route gets more obvious the higher you go.

90. **Z** (5.9) ★ Climb up under the wide crack and undercling around it to gain the left-facing corner.

91. **The Abyss** (5.6) Follow a dorky-looking offwidth in the cave to the right of Z.

92. **Weasel Exit** (5.7) Wide crack going up the flake side of the chimney.

93. **Bushmaster** (5.8) ★ The east face of the cave block has a right-facing corner starting near the ground. Up this to the center of the top block. FA: Don Hynek and Eric Landmann, 1988.

94. **Seduction and Rejection** (5.9) ★★ Take the middle of the three cracks. FA: Eric Landmann and Don Hynek, 1988.

CHIMNEY BUTTRESS—RIGHT

95. **The Horizontal Tango** (5.10) ★ Up the roof 12' right of the previous route, and improvise to the top. FA: Eric Landmann and Don Hynek, 1988.

96. **In and Out** (5.6) ★ Words fail me; check out the photo. This climb must be good practice for something.

97. **Boy Howdy** (5.7) Go farther right, around the corner, to a chimney, etc.

AROMA BUTTRESS

Right of Chimney Buttress and across a shallow gully is a short buttress. Access the top by climbing ledges on the right side, traversing left (south) through a chimney, then stepping across to the main block.

98. **Feeble Men** (5.8+) ★ A black overhang is found on the left-center of the east face. Circle up to it and pull through on small edges.

99. **Stone Edge** (5.9) ★ Start on the right edge of the face and angle up through the small roof to a lichen-covered face.

MINI FORTRESS AREA

From the Prairie Walls area it is possible to walk north, past some short walls and across a shallow gully or two. Alternatively, approach from the fenceline.

FIRST FORTRESS

Access to the left (south).

100. **Surprise Ending** (5.7) ★ On the left side of the higher buttress there is a prominent nose with an overhang at the top. Start where you must to get into the crack.

101. **Dusty Problem** (5.6) There is an alcove to the right of *Surprise Ending*. On the right side is a corner with a roof halfway up. Climb a crack in that corner, then move right onto the nose.

102. **Finger Games** (5.6) ★ The face between the next and previous route.

103. **Fortress Chimney** (5.4) No mystery or excitement here.

L-BUTTRESS

North of First Fortress.

104. **Power Booster** (5.5) At the far-left side of the south face is an offwidth crack in a right-facing corner.

105. **Poison Vines** (5.7) About 6' right of the previous route. Climb to the poison ivy vines and beyond. Maybe it would be smarter to try to put up a harder but safer route to the right.

106. **Hammer** (5.7) On the east face, just right of the large roof.

107. **Loose Rock** (5.7) Up to a ledge about 6' right of *Hammer*. Guess what you'll find on this climb.

FIRST FORTRESS

101

102

L-BUTTRESS

109

110

SQUARE BLOCK BUTTRESS

SPIDERBUSH BUTTRESS

Hike north through some boulders, then slightly uphill. A large oak stands right next to the east face.

108. **Ding Dong** (5.5) Ho Ho. Offwidth.

SQUARE BLOCK BUTTRESS

Downhill from Spiderbush Buttress, around some boulders.

109. **Season's Opener** (5.6) ★ A wide crack on the south side.

110. **Pojama People** (5.10b) ★ Up the east face through a blackish area. Has an interesting move or two.

FORTRESS WALL BUTTRESS

This has an obvious inset. There is a cement foundation about 100 feet below this wall.

111. **Glacier Calf Moo** (5.9) ★ Left of the inset, start on the left edge of a platform. Up the overhanging black cracklet, etc.

112. **Crack Lovers Delight** (5.7) Up the left side of the inset.

113. **Fancy Feet** (5.7) Up the right side of the inset.

BALANCING ROCK AND
SKINNY BUTTRESS

RECEDING RAMPARTS

Moving north along the fenceline about 200 yards from Fortress Wall Buttress, the rock begins to emerge from the trees. Balancing Rock is the first major rock along here and is quite red on the left side. If this area is your goal for the day, park to the north for a shorter approach.

BALANCING ROCK

114. **Double Bucket** (5.6) Start just right of the left-hand roof, then move left to the arete.

115. **Forget-Me-Not** (5.6) Up the right side of the face.

SKINNY BUTTRESS

Thrash north of the small buttress just north of Balancing Rock and lead something—there is no other access to the top.

C-BUTTRESS

Approach the top from either side, but the chimney on the left side (Class 3) is cleaner and better. Be prepared to battle the briars on top.

116. **Hard Start** (5.7+) ★ Follow the face of the mini-buttress on the left side of the main face to the overhang and the top.

117. **The C Direct** (5.6/5.9) ★★ Climb directly up past the right edge of the long overhang (5.6). Variation: *The C* (5.9, no stars) curves in from the left, for some inane reason.

DOMESTIC PILLAR

These are lead routes.

118. **Coach Potato** (5.4) ★ Pick an easy way up the south face of the tower. FA: Eric Landmann and Don Hynek, 1988.

119. **Two Kids and a Honda** (5.8) ★ Up the crack/overhang on the left side of the east face. FA: Don Hynek and Eric Landmann, 1988.

120. **Watching Monday Night Football . . .** (5.5) ★ A crack on the northeast corner leads to easier climbing on the north face. The title was abbreviated. FA: Eric Landmann and Don Hynek, 1988.

POTPOURRI PIECES

121. **Dancin' Fool** (5.9) ★★ There is a large overhang left of *Chockstone Chimney*. At its left edge, climb a crack to a jutting block and outwit it. FA: M. and D. Farris, 1998.

122. **Chockstone Chimney** (5.4) Climb the prominent chimney on the left side. Try not to be the first to pull down all the loose chockstones stacked therein.

123. **Disco Boy** (5.5) ★ Up the face between *Chockstone Chimney* and *Mini Overhang*. The crux involves avoiding the cactus on top. FA: D. and M. Farris, 1998.

DOMESTIC PILLAR

124. **Mini Overhang** (5.6) ★ Up to a triangular overhang and step right. Watch for a loose spot.

125. **Off Balance** (5.8+) ★★ Go straight up the left edge of a black-streaked wall just right of a chimney. Lieback up to a ledge and go up a shallow groove, or step in from the chimney (a bit easier).

TABLE ROCK BUTTRESS

A 20-foot-diameter, flat rock sits about 50 feet from the cliff, providing a nice picnic table and landmark. Please don't throw your trash or orange peels into the grass. A couple of harder climbs make this a more popular destination than most of the buttresses at this end. Approach the top from the right, minimizing erosion.

126. **Don't Give Up** (5.7) ★ Stay left of the roof mentioned below.

127. **Opposing Forces** (5.8) ★ Muscles and gravity. On the left side of the buttress is a small overhang about halfway up. Take the line to the right of the overhang, then up the east face to the top.

128. **Double Chimney** (5.4) ★ As good a place as any to look for bison bones.

129. **Tricky Dick's Galactic Trip** (5.9) ★ Up the face between the cracks on either side.

130. **Prehension** (5.7) ★ Less offwidth than you might imagine, although a little technique is necessary.

TABLE ROCK BUTTRESS

126 · 127 · 128 · 129 · 130 · 131

PROCEEDING
BUTTRESS

135 · 136

131. **Thumbnail Direct** (5.9+) ★★ The bottom is supposed to be harder than the top, but I'm not sure. A thin crack right of *Prehension* doesn't quite reach the ground. Lever up the bottom section, then crunch your bones on the second crux. A rather silly variation traverses into the crack from the right, avoiding the first crux.

PROCEEDING BUTTRESS

132. **Short but Thin** (5.7) ★ In the chimney behind the left side of the buttress is a slightly overhanging crack. Start low, gain a ledge and climb the crack. The nicest climb on the buttress, which is not saying much. FA: M. and D. Farris, 1998.

133. **Cheater's Paradise** (5.7) Thrash up the face just left of a large oak, through briars etc. Avoiding the tree is the crux.

134. **Two Way** (5.7) ★ Climb the crack just left of the large overhang on the left side of the main face. Start on some blocks under an overhang.

135. **Belly Flop Overhang** (5.7-) ★ A hanging, left-facing corner is capped by an overhang. Up the corner, flop over the roof (detached blocks), and so on.

136. **Overhang and Face** (5.7) A short overhanging slot with a tree at the base. Avoid the tree (crux), then climb the face.

137. **Falling Crack** (5.4) ★ On the right side of the buttress is a pointed overhang. A wide crack lies just to the right. Climb it through loose chockstones at the top.

138. **Falling** (5.8) ★ A variation on the previous route, start 5' right and go up to the ledge below the top.

BEGINNER'S BUTTRESS

The northernmost buttress that is worth climbing with a rope. Trees on top for anchors, trees on the bottom for shade, and relatively short and easy routes make this a decent place for kids and other neophytes to learn. It is a bit dirty and has a small amount of loose rock, though.

139. **Beginner's Dihedral** (5.5) ★ Potentially a neat route, but the crack is full of dirt. Use anything you can grab and still stay on the climb.

140. **Beginner's Stairsteps** (5.4) ★ One tricky move at the start leads to 5.0 higher up. A variation (5.8-) goes up the face between this route and the next. It's clean, unlike some routes here.

141. **The Knees Ledge** (5.6) ★ Contrived. Start under the left edge of the big roof and traverse underneath it to the right, around the corner to top.

142. **Beginner's Chimney** (5.4) Mostly face, with back and foot for a couple of moves. Somewhat dirty.

143. **Beginner's Overhang** (5.5) A good way to discourage a real beginner. Up the crack to the overhang, then find a fist jam and stem near the top.

Eric Zschiesche on Berkeley, *Brinton's Buttress.* PHOTO BY DAVE REICH

DEVIL'S LAKE

> I have a healthy disrespect for the rope, which I regard as a link with tradition and a reasonable assurance against the leader falling alone; the stronger the rope, the better his chances of company.
> —TOM PATEY, *The Old Man of Stoerr*

Devil's Lake is the best-known climbing area in the Midwest. The rock is solid quartzite, there are over 1,600 recorded routes to choose from, access is easy, and it's close to Chicago—no wonder it's popular. The Lake has the highest concentration of hard routes in the Upper Midwest, though lack of protection destines most to remain top-rope problems.

As Chris Jones points out in *Climbing in North America*, climbers in a given group tend to have a dress code—the Lake is no exception. The Devil's Lake dress code includes Tevas (or similar sandals), a huge pack, and an optional dog. The first item tells us that access to both the base and top of the cliffline is fairly trivial and isn't very muddy. The second suggests that the approaches to the crags are fairly short. I'm not sure what the third means. The layout of the cliffs does permit easy socialization and there is certainly more of a climbing scene here than at any other area in this guide.

The name "Devil's Lake" deserves some comment. The Winnebago Indians believed the lake was the home of water demons and called it *Ta-wak-cun-chuk-dah* or "Sacred Lake." Another tribe called it *Minnewaukan* or "Evil Spirit Lake." The English name came from Peter Folsom, who in 1842 named it Devils Lake because he thought it looked like the crater of a volcano.

Baraboo is known as the original home of the Ringling Brothers Circus. In 1884 they had their first show, which had three horses and a hyena. The lake was a popular tourist stop over a century ago with lodging and picnic areas at both ends of the lake. The state park was established in 1911, and the area became part of the Ice Age National Scientific Reserve in 1971. Climbers have been using the cliffs for over 70 years. Joe and Paul Stettner began visiting the rocks in the late 1920s and the number of climbers has been increasing ever since.

Emergency contact. Phone the park office at 608-356-8301. If there is no answer, call 911 and ask them to call the park office. The nearest phones for climbs listed in this guide are in the CCC parking lot (East Bluff) and at the boat landing across from the West Bluff parking lot on South Shore Road.

DEVIL'S LAKE OVERVIEW

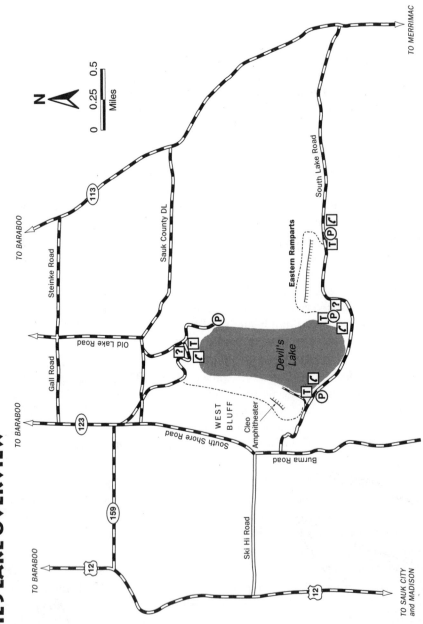

(CCC stands for the Civilian Conservation Corps, which did a lot of work at Devil's Lake in the late 1930s and early 1940s.) There is rescue equipment located on the Eastern Rampart on top of Moldy Buttress, and on the West Bluff above Great Chimney. The nearest hospital is St. Clare Hospital in Baraboo (707 14th Street, Baraboo; 608-356-5561).

The climbing environment: Wisconsin is currently formulating a climbing management plan. Make sure you are aware of any new regulations that arise after the plan is completed.

The *Climber's Guide to Devil's Lake*, by Sven Olof Swartling (1995, University of Wisconsin Press), contains over 1,600 routes and variations on the myriad outcrops scattered throughout the park. The guide is readily available and leads to many fine routes not included here, especially if you are looking for solitude. I have included a selection of the more popular routes on the Eastern Rampart and on the West Bluff in this guide, but be aware that not every climb in these areas is listed here. A handful of minor routes presented here were not given names in Swartling's guide. I've stuck on names that seem appropriate to each climb. First ascent information is taken from *The Hiker's and Climber's Guide to Devil's Lake* (1970), by Smith and Zimmerman, and *The Extremist's Guide to Devil's Lake* (1985), by Leo Hermacinski. Leo deserves the credit for assembling most of this information, and I'll take the heat for any mistakes. Much of the history has been lost, and unless otherwise noted a first ascent is probably on top-rope.

All climbers should obtain a pamphlet from the park entitled *Rock Climbing Safety and Etiquette*. This was produced by the Devil's Lake Climbing Advisory Committee with help from The Access Fund; I'll summarize the critical points here. Carry out all your litter and butts. No bolts or pins are allowed, and climbers are asked to minimize chalk use. Use the bathrooms in the parking lots, and leave the music at home. While you're at it, leave your dog at home too. If Fifi will suffer psychotrauma at home, keep in mind that the park requires your pet to be on a leash (maximum 8 feet) and under control at all times—loose pets may be impounded. Your pet (bark, bark) is not (bark, bark) to interfere with the (bark, bark) enjoyment of others. Finally, crowding is a real problem here. Climb and move on, or let others use your rope.

Devil's Lake and Blue Mounds in Minnesota are geologically very similar. The red quartzite is very solid but lacks friction, especially when wet. There are more cracks at Devil's Lake, and the cliffs are generally taller as well. The routes described here are in areas that attract lots of people, especially on weekends. Solitude can be found if you are willing to explore a little and do shorter routes. See Swartling's guide for the other 1,400 climbs here. Also note that some areas (such as the Sandstone Area) are currently closed to climbing. None of those routes are found in this guide.

Lead climbing at Devil's Lake requires skill and humility. The most important skill is knowing how to place protection in the quartzite. As at Blue Mounds,

Eric Zschiesche on Zschiesche's Roof, *D'Arcy's Wall.* PHOTO BY DAVE REICH

Devil's Lake rock is not friendly to camming devices. Hexes and stoppers, along with the skill to exploit their passive camming abilities, should form the foundation of the new leader's rack. Use longer slings to minimize the chances of loading your pro in unexpected directions. Humility is necessary because most climbs are probably underrated for onsight leads. Don't be proud—back off a grade or two until you get the feel for the friction and pro, and don't even consider leading if the rock is moist.

Services: Baraboo offers all services. While there are many campgrounds in the area, climbers tend to prefer Wheeler's Campground on Wisconsin Highway 159, just northwest of the park (see Appendix A). The campground is open between April Fool's Day and Columbus Day. Camping is available in the state park throughout the year. Climbing equipment is available at Wheeler's Campground and at Sport Haven (see Appendix A). Both are open daily.

Other attractions are too numerous to mention, especially if you are into amusement park and family-oriented activities. Almost anywhere you stop will have brochures describing a few dozen different activities. Of special note in Baraboo are the International Crane Foundation, Circus World Museum, and the Mid-Continent Railway Museum. The Wisconsin Dells lie just a few miles to the north. This world-class tourist trap must be seen to be believed.

Approach: Those coming from the south can take Interstate 90 to Madison and then follow U.S. Highway 12 to Wisconsin Highway 159. Turn right (east) on WI 159 for 1 mile, then go right on WI 123 to South Shore Road. For more freeway driving, stay on I–90 to WI 33 at Portage. Go west on WI 33 to Baraboo, then south on WI 123 to South Shore Road.

From the north or west, exit I–90/94 at US 12 and proceed south about 11 miles. Take WI 159 left (east) at a poorly designed intersection and proceed 1 mile. WI 123 south leads to South Shore Road.

Once on South Shore Road, drive south, then slalom down toward the lake. Parking for West Bluff routes is on the right, immediately after reaching the lakeshore. For East Bluff routes, continue east along the south shore of the lake, past the large parking lot. Cross the railroad tracks (yes, there are trains) and proceed to the parking lot with stone pillars, just east of the Group Camp. There is a gravel lot to your right as you enter, where you should park if possible. Water, toilets, and a phone are available.

Pay your entry fees, as the park authorities check the lots frequently. A self-pay station is available in the East Bluff lot for daily visitors; those visiting the West Bluff should pay at the South Shore ranger station. Regulars should get a season pass or have a federal Golden Eagle card (which is valid both here and at the Wisconsin unit of Interstate State Park).

PEDESTAL BUTTRESS—TOP

BRINTON'S BUTTRESS—TOP

MANY PINES—TOP

MOLDY BUTTRESS—TOP

BILL'S BUTTRESS—TOP

AROUSAL WALL—TOP

PHN—TOP

99

101

HAWK'S NEST—TOP

D'ARCY'S WALL

THE EASTERN RAMPART

The center of action, the climbing crucible, the birthplace of hardmen . . . well, a lot of Tevas and dogs, anyway. Park in the lot east of the group camp; the entrance is marked by stone pillars. Cross the road and proceed directly up the hill on the CCC trail. Switchback through the woods, up the talus, and reach the first rock wall (The Monster). Turn left and ascend the final slope, reaching the base of the main rampart at *Condolences*—a good eye-opener and about a 10- to 15-minute hike. The official trail turns right and quickly attains the top of the cliff. A climber's trail follows the base of the cliff to the west (left).

If you are new to the area, finding the tops of the climbs can be difficult. I've included photos of the tops of the major buttresses to help you get close to your route. Some routes are longer than a doubled rope, so check the ends if you intend to rappel off the taller buttresses (such as Hawk's Nest).

THE MONSTER

The CCC trail ascends to this wall of rocks and turns left. The routes are listed right to left.

1. **Frankenstein** (5.12b) ★ The corner just right of the block.
2. **The Flatiron** (B1) ★★★ Take the center of the 15-foot-high block which rests at the junction of the CCC trail with the rock wall. FA: John Gill (solo), 1962.
3. **The Monster** (5.10c) ★ Up alcove to crack. FL: Peter Cleveland.
4. **The Zipper** (B2) ★ A tight seam just left of a shallow chimney (*The Thing*, 5.7).

D'ARCY'S WALL

This 30-foot buttress is the first rock on the east end of the main cliff line and has a prominent overhang on its east side.

5. **D'Arcy's Wall** (5.8–5.9) ★★★ Start just left of the chimney and work up toward the center of the face, where you finish. FL: Jim Erickson.
6. **Zschiesche's Roof** (V9) ★ Start at the left edge of the face and whimper directly upward. FL: Eric Zschiesche.
7. **Last Gasp** (5.8) ★ Start in the pit just left of the arete. Make several long reaches straight up to the top. FL: Jim Erickson.
8. **Easy Overhang** (5.4) ★ Climb to the prominent ledge right of *Last Gasp*. Traverse 8' right (crux), then trend right to avoid the tree. Not a good lead.
9. **Zig-Zag** (5.5) ★ Gain the ledge noted on the previous climb then battle the tree to follow the left crack.

SOMETIME BLOCK

SOMETIME BLOCK

The next set of routes begins from the top of a large block detached from the main wall.

10. **Sometime Crack Right** (5.10b) ★★ The crack on the right side of the wall. Up to overhang, then cut left.

11. **Sometime Crack** (5.10a) ★★★ A classic crack that is often led (usually after thorough rehearsal). FL: John Gill (solo), 1962.

12. **Sometime Direct** (5.10d) ★★ At the horizontal crack move directly up and flop onto the top. FL: Kurt Krueger, 10/84.

13. **Welfare Line** (5.12b) ★★★ Up the uncompromising face between the surrounding routes.

14. **Sometime Left** (5.11d) ★★ Start on the left side of the wall; at the horizontal crack dodge up and right.

15. **The End** (5.10a) ★★★ Traverse onto the face from blocks inside the chimney.

16. **The End Direct** (5.10b) ★★★ From a pointed block outside the chimney, lunge up to the arrowhead jug and proceed up the normal route. Get tall. FL: Tommy Deuchler.

PEDESTAL BUTTRESS

The cliff just west of Sometime Block.

17. **F4 Ledges** (5.4) ★ Follow the wide crack system to the right of *Birch Tree Crack* and left of the chimney.

18. **The Stretcher** (5.10a) ★★ Another reason to get taller. The face right of *Birch Tree Crack* can be ascended in a number of ways. Pick the easiest, about 10' right of the crack.

19. **Birch Tree Crack** (5.8) ★★ A tricky climb for its grade. Climb the crack, and the crux will find you. Not a good lead for the 5.8 leader.

20. **Hourglass** (5.11c/12a) Forge boldly up the face left of *Birch Tree Crack*. The easier version starts from the alcove in the crack.

21. **Upper Diagonal** (5.9) ★★★ Start at *Birch Tree Crack* and ascend the upper of two diagonal cracks. Often led, but it's not a giveaway. FL: Rich Goldstone.

22. **Lower Diagonal** (5.8) ★★ Follow it to the ledge on the left arete, then follow *Condolences*. FL: Jim Erickson.

23. **The Flake Route** (5.10d) ★★★ A crimp-fest leading directly up the face. Find a thin crack descending from *Upper Diagonal* and climb directly to it. From *Upper Diagonal*, go right a few feet then up, up, up. FL: Steve Sangdahl, 9/80.

PEDESTAL BUTTRESS—FAR RIGHT

24. **The Pedestal** (5.4) ★★ A sinuous route that goes every direction except up. Start on the right side of the pedestal near the left side of the wall. Up this, then cut left to a ledge and a tree. Take the easiest path to the top.

25. **Condolences** (5.7) ★★ Begin on the left side of the pedestal, where the CCC trail descends to the parking lot. Climb the left side to the top of the pedestal, then cut left to the arete. Proceed upward, faking right or left as needed. FL: Jim Erickson.

26. **Congratulations** (5.10a) ★★ The obvious thin crack is popular, partly due to the brevity of the approach. FL: John Gill (solo), 1962.

27. **Ironmongers** (5.8) ★ Start below a right-facing dihedral left of *Congratulations*. Get into the niche, then improvise left and up to trees and the top.

28. **Pine Box** (5.10a) ★ Go straight up from the niche on the previous route. FA: George McHell, 1966. FL: Peter Cleveland.

GILL'S BUTTRESS

The starts of *The Spine* through *Peyote Blues* are reached by clambering 40 feet up a gully left of *Ironmongers*.

29. **The Spine** (5.5) ★★★ A good practice lead, as you can use the chimney wall behind you to make it 5.4. Start from the highest block (with an oak tree), and ascend a dihedral that leans to the left and becomes a chimney. Use the crack only.

GILL'S BUTTRESS—LEFT

30. **Acid Rock** (5.12a) ★★★ Start 12' left of *The Spine* on a small ledge on the main wall. Climb up a few feet, then do a diagonal, leftward traverse to a small ledge near the left edge. Meander back right, finishing in the center of the narrowing wall. FA: Peter Cleveland and Steve Wunsch.

31. **Slut for Punishment** (5.12a) ★★ Go straight up instead of traversing left as on *Acid Rock*. FA: Steve Sangdahl, 1982.

32. **Peyote Blues** (5.12b) ★★ From the left edge of the block at the base of *Acid Rock*, fall across the gap to a handhold. Work up a flake and edges just right of *Gill's Nose*. FA: Rich Bechler(?).

33. **Ice** (5.13a) ★★ Start in the chimney and gain the *Peyote Blues* start from below. FA: Dave Groth.

34. **Gill's Nose** (5.11b/c) ★★★ Start just right of the *Boy Scout* slab and power up the left side of the rounded arete. FL: Tommy Deuchler.

35. **Gill's Cheek** (5.12a) ★★★ Between *Gill's Nose* and *Gill's Crack*. If you have a good hold, you're probably off route.

36. **Gill's Crack** (5.10b) ★★★ Up the slab to the crack, up the crack to the top. FA: John Gill (solo), 1962.

BRINTON'S BUTTRESS

37. **Boy Scout** (5.4) ★★ The obvious slab between Gill's and Brinton's Buttresses. Wander up the slab, then climb the chimney at the top for a schizophrenic climb.

38. **Rubber Man** (5.13b) ★★★ Start at the top of the slab, in the center of the face above, and mantle your way to glory. FA: Eric Zschiesche.

39. **Cheap Thrills** (5.12b/c) ★★ Start at the left edge of the top of the slab and stay right of the small inside corner. FA: Dave Erickson(A3); FFA: Peter Cleveland.

40. **Chiaroscuro** (5.9+) Start right of *Brinton's Crack* and left of the corner. Climb directly up to the right side of the traverse on the next route.

41. **Brinton's Crack** (5.6) ★★★ Jack Fralick (who witnessed the first ascent) says that Fritz Wiessner backed off the lead that day, then Bob Brinton made the attempt. At the crux, Brinton faltered, hung at full extension, then successfully cranked through the moves. FL: Bob Brinton, 1942.

42. **Brinton's Direct** (5.9) ★★ Go straight up instead of traversing right. FL: Peter Cleveland.

43. **Brinton's Corner** (5.10a) ★ Stay on the left corner.

44. **Rococo Variations** (5.7) Start near the right edge and clamber up to join *Berkeley*. FL: Jim Erickson.

45. **Berkeley** (5.6+) ★★ Finding the easiest route may take some work. Up the crack, move right under roof, zigzag to the top. FL: Steve Roper.

Terry Kieck on Brinton's Crack. PHOTO BY DAVE REICH

BRINTON'S BUTTRESS—RIGHT

BRINTON'S BUTTRESS—LEFT

TWO PINES BUTTRESS—RIGHT

46. **Chicago** (5.8+) ★ Do the initial crack on *Berkeley* then zoom up and a bit left. FL: Jim Erickson.

47. **Evanston Township** (5.10a) ★ Parallel *Chicago*, staying a few feet left. FA: Peter Cleveland.

TWO PINES BUTTRESS

48. **The Rack** (5.7) ★★ Curve up and right to stance, then back left to corner.

49. **Crosstown Traffic** (5.12a) ★ Use only the right-hand crack of *Thoroughfare*. FL: Rich Bechler, 1982.

50. **Thoroughfare** (5.11a) ★★★ Climb an inside corner just right of the chimney. Use both cracks all the way up. FL: Scott Stewart, 1971.

51. **Vacillation** (5.7+) ★ A thin crack/corner a few feet left of the chimney

52. **Mouse's Tail** (5.11c) ★ Up *Mouse's Misery* until your feet are even with the triangular roof. Move right, lieback up the arch, then move up and avoid any useful holds. FA: Ralph Schmitt ca. 1978. FL: Steve Sangdahl, 1982.

53. **Mouse Tracks** (5.11a) ★★ Above the arched roof is a pair of elongated pockets. Climb *Mouse's Misery*, angle up to the center of the roof, then lever up through the pockets.

54. **Mouse's Misery** (5.10a/b) ★★★ Up the face a few feet left of *Vacillation* and evade the overhang via the crack at its left edge. FL: Jim Erickson, 1966 (with a bolt).

55. **Full Stop** (5.6) ★★★ Up the thin crack to a flake, then cut left and up to the tree-filled gully.

56. **Big Deal** (5.9+) ★ Go straight up from the flake. FL: Peter Cleveland.

57. **Reprieve** (5.7) ★ Wander up the face between *Full Stop* and the corner.

58. **Schizophrenia** (5.6) ★ At the toe of the buttress a jagged crack leads to a dark overhang 20' up. Climb this crack, pass around either side of the overhang, and amble up the ridge.

59. **Moderation** (5.4) ★ Start 15' left of *Schizophrenia*, diagonal right to a point above the dark roof, and continue up the ridge.

MANY PINES BUTTRESS

60. **Anemia** (5.2) ★★ The low-angle crack system left of the large dihedral.

61. **Peter's Project** (5.7) ★★ A thin crack works through a bulge on the left side of the face. Flow up this, then wander up the pleasant face above. A bit loose in spots.

62. **Ostentation** (5.10a) ★ Start 6' left of *Peter's Project*, beneath the overhang. Climb up to the overhang, go around it slightly left of the nose, then back right. Continue up just right of the nose.

TWO PINES BUTTRESS—LEFT

MANY PINES BUTTRESS—RIGHT

MANY PINES BUTTRESS—LEFT

63. **Callipigeanous Crack** (5.10a) ★ About 7' right of *Michael's Project* is a thin crack. Zip up this to a stance, then move right to the corner. FL: Jim Erickson.

64. **Asleep in a Fuknes Dream** (5.12a) ★ Start just left of the previous route and go straight up the rounded nose above. FA: Tommy Deuchler.

65. **No Trump** (5.11d) Stay an arm's length right of *Michael's Project* and don't use the crack. You may need a referee to distinguish between this route and the previous one. FL: Barry Rugo (solo), 1981.

66. **Michael's Project** (5.8) ★ Plod up the crack for about 15' then lunge right to a friendly flake. Go back to the main crack and thrutch up to the top.

67. **Flatus** (5.11b) ★★ Start on *Black Rib* and diagonal up and right. Cut left at the overhang. FL: Peter Cleveland.

68. **Flatus Direct** (5.11d) ★ Stay right at the bottom, or at the top, or both. Both the start and finish are 5.11d.

69. **Black Rib** (5.11a) ★★ Try to figure out the easiest start, then climb the rib to the chimney. FL: Peter Cleveland.

70. **Double Clutch** (5.12a) ★ The really blank face left of *Black Rib*.

71. **Man and Superman** (5.10d) ★ The somewhat blank rib left of *Double Clutch*; cut left at the top. FA: Peter Cleveland.

MOLDY BUTTRESS

Rescue equipment is found on top of this buttress.

72. **Cul-de-Sac** (5.8) ★ Up the corner and go right around the roof.

73. **Fibula Cracks** (5.12b) ★ Just left of the previous route is a short corner capped by a small roof. Go straight up above and pass the upper roof on the right.

74. **Tibia Crack** (5.8) ★ About 10' left of *Cul-de-Sac* is a crack leading to a V-slot 40' up.

BILL'S BUTTRESS

75. **Breakfast of Champions** (5.8+) ★ To the right of *Cheatah* is a gully/V-chimney. On the left wall, 6' left of the corner, is a hand crack. Climb it, then up and left as needed.

76. **Ignominy** (5.4) ★ Wander up the easiest route left of the previous climb.

77. **Tiger** (5.12a) ★★★ Just right of *Cheatah*, and don't use the jug.

78. **Cheatah** (5.10b) ★★★ Somebody is always on this, and for good reason. Forge more or less straight up.

79. **Push-Mi, Pull-Yu** (5.6) ★★★ Real fun. Up the crack past a dead pine.

MOLDY BUTTRESS

80. **Agnostic** (5.7) ★★ Into an alcove, step to a ledge, then straight up.

81. **Mr. Bunney Meets the Poultry Man** (5.11a) ★★ Climb the wall right of *Coatimundi Crack* through the overhang at the top.

82. **Coatimundi Crack** (5.6+) ★★★ Just left of the toe of the buttress is a prominent crack/V-groove. Climb it, go past a ledge, and up to an outside corner on the left. Do this or move left.

RAINY WEDNESDAY TOWER

Don't hesitate to provide a belay when ascending or descending the summit. Take a short chimney on the northeast side of the tower.

83. **False Alarm Jam** (5.6) ★★ Locate a prominent crack halfway up the right side of the tower. Scamper up to this, climb it, and proceed to the top.

84. **Resurrection** (5.10a) ★★ The south face of Rainy Wednesday Tower has a large ledge about 12' up. From that ledge, climb the right-center of the face, easing your way left to the scoop beneath the overhang. Exit to the right.

85. **Double Overhang** (5.4) ★★ A major left-facing corner is found on the south face. Climb this, slither left, then weave up through the overhang above.

**RAINY WEDNESDAY
TOWER—RIGHT**

AROUSAL WALL

The wall just east of Leaning Tower Gully.

86. **Cerebration** (5.4) ★ The large left-facing corner.

87. **Second Coming** (5.7) ★ Up the face to a ledge. At some point work left to the top.

88. **Orgasm Direct** (5.11b) ★★ Stay a few feet right of the corner and forge boldly upward. FL: Rich Bechler, 1980.

89. **Orgasm** (5.8) ★★ Gain the inside corner beneath the large roof and exit right.

90. **Foreplay** (5.6) ★ Start in the crack left of the previous route, go up, move right, etc. Loose at top.

PSEUDO HAWK'S NEST

The large, multifaceted buttress west of the Leaning Tower Gully. The tops of most routes are accessed from the gully itself. Routes such as *Death and Disfiguration* are reached from the highest ledge on the west wall (Class 3 downclimb to pine tree ledge). *Epiphany* through *Hero's Fright* can be reached from the squat tower or the ledge just below. *Pretzel* is set up from the yellowish, flat ledge about 40 feet from the bottom of the gully.

91. **The Pretzel** (5.6) ★★ The first left-facing corner as one descends west from the base of the Leaning Tower Gully. Look like Mr. Salty, resorting to technique when necessary.

PSEUDO HAWK'S NEST—RIGHT

92. **Drunken Sailor** (5.6+) ★★ Ascend a few feet on ledges just right of *Epiphany*. Launch up to the square-cut ledge on the arete above. After gaining the slab, you can climb it any way you choose. FL: Tom Duwiddie.

93. **Epiphany** (5.9+) ★ Right of the next route is a thinner crack. Follow this upward without using the left wall of the dihedral. When you've had enough, exit up and right.

94. **Cracking Up** (5.5) A wider crack in a right-facing dihedral. Work up this, looking for the crux.

95. **Bagatelle** (5.12d) ★★★ The wall left of *Cracking Up* has two thin intermittent cracks/seams. This is the right line. Imagine leading it. FA: Peter Cleveland. FL: Tommy Deuchler, 1981.

96. **Phlogiston** (5.13b) ★★ *The Extremist's Guide* says, "The second ascent still awaits the man with enough determination and spare time." The second ascent was accomplished by Lynn Hill after a few tries. FA: Jay Stewart and Bill Campbell; FFA: Peter Cleveland.

97. **Beginner's Demise** (5.11a) ★★ Stay quite close to the right edge of the east face, up a flake-like affair through the bulge, and up more steep rock above. FA: Peter Cleveland.

98. **ABM** (5.11b) ★★ This route takes the left-center of the wall.

PSEUDO HAWK'S NEST—CENTER

99. **Chicken Delight** (5.7) ★★ There is a sharp rib about 12' up. Stay right of this, up the corner, and proceed more or less straight up. Protects OK, but may require some thought.

100. **Beginner's Delight** (5.4) ★★★ Take any of several variations up the southwest corner of the buttress.

101. **Hero's Fright** (5.7) ★★ A crack is visible on the wall between the previous route and the chimney. Climb up any old way and do the crack. FL: Jim Erickson.

102. **Death and Transfiguration** (5.5) ★ A 3' chimney splits two tall blocks just left of a larger chimney/gully. Scamper up the chimney and a short, steep wall above the blocks. A right-facing corner takes you through an overhang to a ledge. Setup: The ledge can be accessed from Leaning Tower Gully.

103. **Death and Disfiguration** (5.8) ★★ Climb the left block mentioned in the previous route and do the thin crack up to the tree.

104. **Degrade My Sister** (5.11a) ★★ Up the face right of the rib. Finish a few feet left of the tree.

105. **Prime Rib** (5.9+) ★★ Up the rib, then slightly left to the top.

106. **Bloody Mary** (5.8) ★★ A corner leads to a dark roof. Take the crack through the roof, then head for the ledge left of the corner.

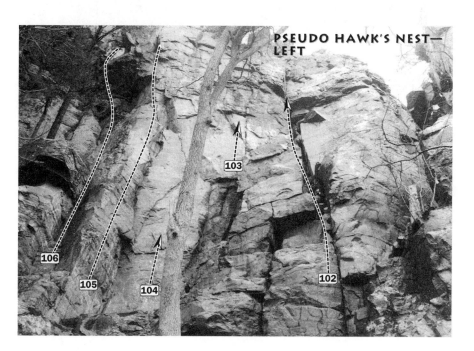

PSEUDO HAWK'S NEST—LEFT

HAWK'S NEST—FAR RIGHT

HAWK'S NEST—CENTER

HAWK'S NEST

These are long routes and the setups are not always obvious from above. The last few routes can be set up by descending the gully just west of the buttress to the lowest ledge that is easily accessible. This ledge can also be reached from below. Walk left of the large block at the base of *Coronary* to a left-slanting gully or chimney. Climb this, then cut up and right over a short wall (Class 3) to a broken area. Work right to the bed of the gully and then to the ledge.

107. **Happy Hunting Grounds** (5.11a) ★★ Up the thin crack just right of some blocks and through the right side of the overhang at the top.

108. **Flakes Away** (5.12a) ★ Imagine a route a few feet left of the previous climb.

109. **Double Hernia** (5.12a) ★ Follow a thin crack to a ledge and continue to the right of the corner.

110. **Bucket Brigade** (5.6) ★★ Climb the easy-looking crack/corner, then follow the right-hand branch. Setup: Work as low as possible down the left-center to a bushy tree. FL: Sheldon Smith.

111. **The Ramp** (5.6) ★★ Same start as *Bucket Brigade*, but follow the left-hand branch. Many variations are possible here.

112. **No Fruit Please/Pieplate** (5.11b) ★ These two routes use the face left of the previous route. You try to tell them apart.

113. **Vivisection** (5.11a) ★★ A short right-facing corner leads to a roof, a face, a roof, and cracks, more or less in that order. FA: Peter Cleveland.

HAWK'S NEST—LEFT

114. **Alpha Centauri** (5.10d) ★★ Take the wall left of *Vivisection* to avoid the crux on that route. FL: Jim Erickson.

115. **Anomie** (5.8) ★ Up a short dihedral, then wander up and right.

116. **Charybdis** (5.7) ★★★ A fine climb. Take a crack right of the large block and follow cracks up and right.

117. **Scylla** (5.7) ★★ Start as for *Charybdis*, then trend left to the right-facing corner above.

118. **Coronary** (5.7+) ★★ From the top of the block, climb up and right to a ledge. Fake back left and up on some questionable blocks through the roof.

THE WEST BLUFF

There are many climbs on the West Bluff, enough for some solitude on a busy weekend. You'll need to consult Swartling's guide to find those routes, however. The routes described here are located near the first major overlook along the trail. Park in the gravel lot on the south side of the road at the southwest corner of the lake. Hike up the paved steps and follow the trail for 10–15 minutes. Expect these to be busy, as the access is pretty easy.

CLEO AMPHITHEATER

This area is the first major overlook on the West Bluff Trail. The rightmost overlook is above Tilted Tower; *The Plank* lies just to the left. The prow of *King's Throne* is visible to the north, and Cleopatra's Needle is visible downhill and slightly north. The base of the climbs can most easily be reached by downclimbing a chimney just south of *King's Throne*. A grungy downclimb can also be done due south of this chimney, near where you first reach the overlook.

Erosion is a problem in the descent gully. Weave back and forth along the lower-angle areas to minimize soil loss. Remember, parts of Interstate State Park were closed to climbing by Wisconsin officials for this very reason.

119. **Barndoor** (5.8) A crack directly south of *The Plank*, right of Tilted Tower.

120. **Dumb Wide Crack** (5.4) ★ Up the obvious wide crack. The face just to the right is 5.8-.

121. **The Plank** (5.9+) ★ Start up the wide crack, then traverse right immediately above the overhang and try to go up the crack.

122. **Hang Dog** (5.9+) Climb to an alcove, then up through a slimy crack to the top.

Right (south) of the top of *King's Throne* a ledge curves around right to the descent chimney. The next four routes end on this ledge.

123. **Curved Wall** (5.7) ★ On the rounded buttress of the descent gully, left of *Mickey Mouse*. Up to a ledge, then left and up.

CLEO AMPHITHEATER—TOP

THE PLANK AREA

124. **Mickey Mouse** (5.4) ★ There are two short cracks that start off of a ledge. This is the left one.

125. **Minnie Mouse** (5.4) ★ The right crack.

126. **Minnie Mum** (5.2) ★ The inside corner.

127. **Missing Link** (5.10a) ★ If you can find the 5.8 version, let me know. On the right wall of the *Minnie Mum* corner are a couple of ledges. Go from ledge to ledge to top.

128. **King's Throne** (5.6) ★★ An obvious prow from above. Climb just left of a wide crack up the east-facing prow. Reachy and probably harder for short people.

129. **Throne Room** (5.5) ★ The wide crack right of *King's Throne*. Finish on the north or east face.

130. **Queen's Throne** (5.4) ★★★ A stellar lead at its grade. Climb the right-hand of two left-facing corners to the right of *King's Throne*, ending just right of a tall rock spike.

131. **Queen's Face** (5.8) ★ Climb the face east of *Queen's Throne* without using the edges. You can force a slightly harder climb to the left of this route.

CLEOPATRA'S NEEDLE

Descend by downclimbing or by rappelling a single line running over the top of the needle. Quality ratings reflect the unique position rather than exceptional climbing.

CLEOPATRA'S
NEEDLE—NORTH

CLEOPATRA'S
NEEDLE—SOUTH

133

135

WIESSNER WALL—TOP

WIESSNER WALL

TURK'S HEAD

132. **Southeast Side** (5.4) ★★ Start on the northeast corner, traverse left, and gallop up to the summit block. Finish on the southeast or north sides.

133. **Northwest Side** (5.4) ★★ From the uphill (west) side, ascend ledges up and left.

134. **North Ledges** (5.4) ★★ Up the north face.

135. **Southwest Rib** (5.7) ★★ Climb the rib directly, or up the crack to its left.

WIESSNER WALL

Follow trails north of the Cleo Amphitheater for about 50 yards. Once on the north side of a rocky ridge that runs east, hike east to the top of the climbs. Reach the base of the wall by descending north down gullies, or approach from Cleopatra's Needle.

136. **The Wasp** (5.8) ★★ All the right footholds are missing. Start on large blocks at far-left end of wall. Easily climb the corner, traverse right around an overhang. Step up into the crack (crux) and proceed to the large ledge.

137. **Fritz** (5.7) ★★ Start in a discontinuous crack 8' left of *Stinger*. A short way up, traverse left to a thin crack and up to the ledge. Continue if you wish, but beware of loose blocks in the cracks above the alcove.

138. **Stinger** (5.8) ★★ Just left of *Wiessner Chimney* is an alcove 15' up. Climb up to the alcove, step left, then back right to gain the tree. Continue with *Wiessner Face*.

WIESSNER WALL

139. **Wiessner Chimney** (5.4) ★★★ Up the chimney right of the alcove, then get onto a slab and traverse to the tree. Continue up the 5.3 crack above. Belay in a position that avoids damaging the tree.

140. **Just another Pretty Face** (5.10a–5.11a) ★ Start just right of the block at the base of the chimney. Go straight up the face (5.11) or traverse up and left to the very edge of the chimney then up to the slab (5.10a).

141. **Wiessner Face** (5.7) ★★ From the tree on the midway ledge, climb up and right, then more or less straight up on positive holds to the top.

Keith Anderson on Mississippi Burning, *Barn Bluff.*

Red Wing

Barn Bluff, an old quarry site near downtown Red Wing, is the perfect location for a sport climbing area. Climbers have used Barn Bluff in Red Wing for many years, but the effort needed to set up top-ropes was so great that few could stomach more than an occasional visit. A bolting campaign by a few individuals has turned the cliff into a sport-climbing area that has seen heavy use in the 1990s.

While bolts are often portrayed as environmentally destructive, in this case they probably have reduced the potential damage to the cliff system. The sloping, loose material that caps the cliff would be seriously eroded (and would send an endless stream of debris down onto climbers) if the same number of climbers set up top-ropes. The area is owned by the City of Red Wing.

Emergency contact: Dial 911, but self-rescue if possible. The nearest hospital is the Fairview Red Wing Hospital, 1407 West 4th Street, Red Wing, (651-388-6721).

The climbing environment: The access situation here seems to be somewhat stable, but it will only take one bad accident to reopen this issue. Other factors can affect access, and these can be controlled by all of us. Pick up all trash, including that of non-climbers. Use the toilets in town. Remove all gear from climbs (webbing, quickdraws). Camouflage fixed gear by painting it or by buying colored hangers.

The northern exposure of much of the cliff combines with the porous nature of the rock to yield rock that is often damp, especially at the bottom. The southern exposure is much drier and can offer decent climbing conditions when the north side is either too cold or wet. The main creatures of note at the bluff are rattlesnakes, bats, and the ubiquitous mosquitos.

There is a significant amount of loose rock on Barn Bluff, both on the routes and above the climbs. To reduce the chance of pulling off a hold, apply force to the hold in the appropriate direction (down, and not out). Helmets are strongly encouraged for leaders, belayers, and spectators. Avoid belaying in the fall line. If nonclimbers stop to rubberneck, try to persuade them to move out of the line of fire. Pigeons and squirrels can dislodge materials as well.

Prospective leaders should also keep in mind that the rating of a climb can change dramatically if even one hold disintegrates, which is not an uncommon event here. This same deciduous, porous rock also houses the protection system for most climbs (the bolts). These bolts are starting to age, so think twice before taking an excessive number of unnecessary falls—come back another day when

RED WING OVERVIEW

WISCONSIN

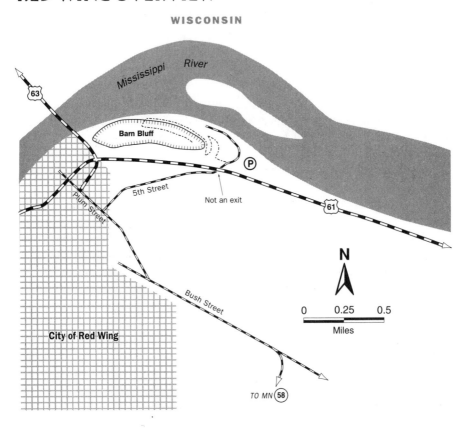

you are in better form. Finally, remember that you are looking at a ground fall if you blow the second clip on many routes. Double-rope technique can help minimize this potential problem if you are climbing at the edge of your ability. Stick-clip the first bolt or two if you feel it is necessary, or climb an easier route.

The leads at Red Wing generally don't end at the top of the cliff. The fixed anchors at the tops of most of the routes can provide you with a stupid way to die. **Many of the top anchors are dangerously worn.** Both cold shuts and carabiners need to be replaced. The only folks who can fix this are those who are climbing the routes today. Take some time and help maintain these climbs by improving the anchors when needed. Also, keep your waist below open hooks when starting to lower, and don't drop the rope! The open hooks should be replaced with more modern and safer stations by those with the knowledge to do so.

Chipping, gluing, and retrobolting are not part of the local ethic. In fact, they are inappropriate anywhere. Also, think carefully before adding new bolts. Routes are getting pretty close together in a number of spots.

I have not generally provided gear recommendations for these routes, so count the bolts or look at the crack. Carrying a couple of extra quickdraws is recommended. New climbs are being added all the time, so check the photos and verbal descriptions carefully to make sure you're on the right route. Nate Postma's *Barnyard Boogie* was the first guide to the area. Some routes were included in *Minnesota Rock: Selected Climbs*. I have included all known routes as of October 1999 in this guide.

Services: There are no restrooms or other facilities at the bluff. Since a lot of non-climbers are walking around, find a secluded spot in which to deal with bodily concerns (there has been some talk of improving these facilities in the future). The city of Red Wing offers any other service you are likely to need.

There is currently no climbing shop in Red Wing. The Twin Cities area offers a number of climbing shops. Midwest Mountaineering, Vertical Endeavors, and P.J. Asch Otterfitters are locally owned. Chain stores include REI (Bloomington and Roseville) and Eastern Mountain Sports (Burnsville). In Rochester, gear is available at Prairie Walls Climbing Gym. (See Appendix A for more information.)

Approach: Barn Bluff is located north of U.S. Highway 61 in downtown Red Wing, just east of the US 63 bridge over the Mississippi River. It is not accessible from US 61, however. The best approach is to take either US 61 or 63 to Plum Street (Minnesota Highway 58). Proceed southeast on Plum and turn left (northeast) on East Fifth Street. Jog right, staying on Fifth Street, pass underneath US 61, and park in the provided area across from the steps. Those coming to Red Wing from the south on MN 58 eventually find themselves on Plum Street and turn right on Fifth Street.

Please use the trail system, and avoid taking shortcuts. You really don't save any time and your erosional activities will only make it more difficult to maintain climbing access. It takes all of about 7 minutes to follow the maintained trail to the base of *Barnburner*—not what I would call a horrid approach (especially with those itty-bitty sport racks).

The cliff is logically divided into south and north faces, with the east end in between. The routes are described in a counterclockwise (left to right) direction, starting with the westernmost climbs on the south face. The described climbs are located in eight discrete areas on these faces. Once an area is located, individual climbs are best found by using the pictures and looking for the top anchors (chains or hooks). For simplicity, I assume that the trails run due east and west.

The stairs across from the parking area are the start of the approach. Hike up the stairs, staying to the right, around to the north side of the rock. Pass buckthorn, sumac, and red oaks, then switchback left and up. Stay on the main trail, and reach an intersection near the base of the rock. At this point a major crack/corner (*Jam and Jelly*) is directly in front of you behind a birch. The crack of *Barnburner* is near the right margin of this face, which is the right end of The

RED WING DETAIL

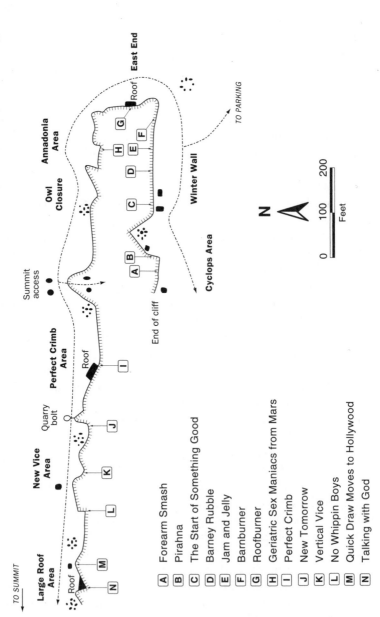

A Forearm Smash
B Pirahna
C The Start of Something Good
D Barney Rubble
E Jam and Jelly
F Barnburner
G Roofburner
H Geriatric Sex Maniacs from Mars
I Perfect Crimb
J New Tomorrow
K Vertical Vice
L No Whippin Boys
M Quick Draw Moves to Hollywood
N Talking with God

Winter Wall. The Winter Wall extends left (west) of *Barnburner* for about 250 feet, ending at a scree pile. Left of this scree pile is the Cyclops Area (named for the large hole in the rock).

Returning to *Barnburner*, The East End is the obvious, wide prow right of *Barnburner*. The right edge of this prow is formed by a six-foot-wide buttress of black rock. The right side of this buttress marks the start of the Annadonia Area. The trail is slightly elevated here and is separated from the rock by a small talus area. The Annadonia Area ends at a protruding gray buttress just left of a lieback flake.

The gray buttress marks the start of the Owl Closure Area, which stretches to the scree pile about 70 feet farther along the trail. No climbing is allowed in this area from February through June. Approximately 200 feet past the scree pile, the trail passes close to some large boulders leading up to a break in the cliff system. The top can be reached from here, although the slope is deteriorating rapidly from short-sighted scramblers. Stay on rocks and avoid going straight up when possible.

Another 175 feet takes you to The Perfect Crimb Area, which is identified by a large roof 20 feet up. The trail then passes very close to a buttress containing an old quarry bolt, which marks the left edge of The New Vice Area. Many of the climbs in this area are found past a scree slope and near the next major rock wall close to the trail. The Large Roof Area is found about 120 yards beyond the quarry bolt at (not surprisingly) a large roof. Just right of the roof is a scree pile that marks the end of the climbs.

THE CYCLOPS AREA

As you move left of the *Barnburner* area the cliffs decline, ending in a small tower with some ledges to its right. The Cyclops Area lies between this tower and the scree slope to the right. The main crack is *Forearm Smash*, and the large hole near the top is The Cyclops Eye.

1. **Sobriety** (5.10-) There is at least one route that starts from the pedestal to the left of the next route. Really trashy. FA: Nate Postma, 1992.

2. **User Friendly** (5.12b) ★ Two-bolt start, a few feet left of *Wasp Mentality*. FA: Mike Dahlberg.

3. **Unknown** (5.10?) A possible top-rope between *User Friendly* and *Wasp Mentality*.

4. **Wasp Mentality** (5.11c) ★★★ Tricky and fun, but watch for wasps in the undercling. Start about 3' left of *Cooler Crack* and try to follow a line of bolts to a set of open hooks at the top, just below the birch tree. FA: Mike Dahlberg.

5. **Forearm Smash, a.k.a. Cooler Crack** (5.8) ★ A 4- to 5-inch crack at the bottom. Solid pro for competent leaders, an unwise choice for others.

CYCLOPS AREA

6. **Work Ethic** (5.12a) ★★★ You need one to be successful on this sustained route. About 6' right of *Forearm Smash*, proceed directly up to hooks. FA: Mike Dahlberg.

7. **Suicide Squeeze** (5.11c) ★★★ Between *Work Ethic* and *Cyclops*. FA: Dan Meyer, 1990.

8. **Cyclops** (5.12a) ★★★ Here comes ol' one-eye! Directly below The Cyclops Eye is a line of bolts. A combination of a brief crux and the eye makes for fun, balancy climbing. FA: Mike Dahlberg.

9. **Sleeping Bat in a Ziplock Bag** (5.10a) ★★★ A good but deciduous route. Take a long runner for the clip under the overhang. About 8' right of *Cyclops*, start just left of a whitish face. From the ledge sneak left and climb just right of the eye. A direct finish (*End Play*, 5.11) is possible if desired. FA: Mike Dahlberg.

10. **Urban Chunks** (5.11a) ★ Start 7' right of the previous route, just left of the outside corner. Climb interesting pockets and knobs (watch the 2nd clip), then trend slightly right and up a blunt arete to the big chains. Cleaned and drilled by Dahlberg as *Urban Renewal*, then climbed by Engel as *Captain Chunks*, hence the name. FA: Mike Dahlberg and Jeff Engel.

11. **Big Rocks Remembered** (5.11d) ★★ Six feet right of *Urban Chunks*, just right of a blunt nose. FA: Pam Postma and Nate Postma, 1992.

12. **Piranha** (5.12b) Seven feet right of the previous route, in the middle of the face. Would be better with more traffic. FA: Mike Dahlberg.

13. **Pigeon Paranoia** (5.10-) Five feet right of *Piranha* and 4' left of the large block against the wall. The first bolt is missing. FA: Jeff Engel.

THE WINTER WALL

Starting right of the scree pile, the wall faces southwest for a few yards, then curves around to face almost directly south. It extends for about 80 yards to *Barnburner*, where the cliff turns and faces east. The three major cracks in the right half of this area and some talus blocks at the base of the climbs provide landmarks for locating the routes.

14. **Orange Marmalade** (5.12) ★ Start by climbing up on a ledge rising to the left of *Relentless*. Work up the line of bolts that rises above the highest point of this ledge. There are 3 anchors at the top. FA: Josh Helke, 6/98.

15. **Skooter Trash** (5.11b) This old line starts in the same vicinity as the previous route then cuts right and finishes in the vicinity of the next route, staying left of *Relentless*. FA: Nate Postma, 1991.

16. **Longing for Miss Adonis** (5.12a) ★ About 10' left of *Relentless*. Follow 3 bolts up to a hueco then up the left side of the upper dihedral. FA: Josh Helke, Jeremy Mariette, and Mike Helke, 1998.

RELENTLESS AREA—LEFT

Chris Minson on The Start of Something Good. PHOTO BY JOHN HALLIWILL

17. **Relentless** (5.11) ★★★ Top-rope time on this well-named crack. To the right of the scree pile, find an obvious thin crack that goes up, angles left, then up again. A direct finish straight up is 5.12+ (Lowe Balls, etc. on lead). FA: of Direct: Mike Dahlberg.

18. **Meet The Feebles** (5.?) This is an open project 5' right of *Relentless*. The first bolt is above a small roof.

19. **NSP** (5.13+?) Four feet right of previous climb, the first bolt is above a small crescent in the rock. A crucial hold at the crux has fallen off, and the current rating is not known. FA: Keith Anderson. Bolted and nearly climbed by Tom Ramier.

20. **Projects** (5.?) There are two open projects here; one is 14' right of previous climb and trends left at top. The other is not bolted and lies to the left of the first project. Look for a lone bolt about 20' up.

21. **Soft Touch** (5.12b) ★ A line of bolts drops down almost directly from the dihedral right on the corner between the two faces. FTR: Mike Dahlberg; FL: Nate Postma, 1988.

22. **Right Touch** (5.12b) This variation connects to *New Kids . . .* after the crux on *Soft Touch*. FA: Mike Dahlberg.

23. **New Kids on the Rock** (5.10d) ★ People seem to love or hate this route. Just left of a faint outside corner, 15' left of the following climb. There is a small ledge about 6' up. Stay right of the arete at the top for a pure ascent.

24. **Jump Start** (5.10a-c) ★ About 75' right of *Relentless*, the wall curves, and there is a six-foot-tall block next to the wall. Just left of this block are some bolts. Bounce up to the small ledge about 11' up. Continue to a tricky traverse about halfway up, and watch for loose stuff near the top. A bolt connects this route to the next one to form *Jump to Something Good*.

25. **The Start of Something Good** (5.12a) ★★ If you can start it, you're good. Consistent 5.11 huecos and edges to the finish; it's long and pumpy. This route starts from the block, angles right, and ends right of the woody bushes at the top. FA: Mike Dahlberg.

26. **Squeeze Play** (5.12) From previous route, up past its crux, take a hard right to the hueco, then up. FA: Mike Dahlberg.

27. **A Drilling Experience** (5.11c) ★★ Any holes in your technique will be exposed by this climb. Twenty-five feet right of the block marking the previous routes is a one-foot-high, 5' x 2' block. This route starts left of this block, under the left side of the small overhang at a yellow flake. A low crux and a spooky 5.9 left-rising traverse await you. FA: Mike Dahlberg.

28. **Preemptive Strike** (5.12c) ★★★ Just left of *Barney Rubble* is a very fine route. FA: Mike Dahlberg.

BARNEY RUBBLE
AREA

29. **Barney Rubble, a.k.a. Birch Tree Crack** (5.9) The leftmost of the three continuous cracks on the south face.

30. **Pretty in Pink** (5.10) Use *Barney Rubble* until the crack splits about half-way, then right, following the bolts. Bring gear for the crack down low. FA: Pam Postma and Nate Postma, 1990.

31. **Toxic Art** (5.11a) This route somehow uses the crack, then breaks out right below *Pretty in Pink*. FA: Nate Postma, 1990.

32. **Vias, a.k.a. Godzilla** (5.12c) ★ Locate a hueco, reachable from the ground, to the right of *Barney Rubble*. Climb up to the second bolt and take the left-hand line.

33. **Last Dance of the Fat Man** (5.12d/13a) ★ Start at the hueco and take the right-hand line. FA: Jeremy Mariette and Keith Anderson.

34. **Rock Pigs** (5.12c/d) ★★★ Right of the previous route's hueco is a bolt just left of a tight flake that looks something like a baby elephant's foot. Straight up. FA: Nate Postma, 1989.

35. **Light My Fire** (5.12c/d) ★★ A two-finger pocket leads to a seam and undercling. FA: Jeff Engel.

36. **Project** (5.?) This project goes up the line of bolts just left of the next climb.

37. **Kelly's Arete** (5.12a) ★ The bolt line just left of the arete. Start in *Jam and Jelly*, using the crack to the first bolt. FA: Kelly Gorder.

38. **Jam and Jelly** (5.7) ★ The center of the three obvious cracks in this face. Good pro if you know what you are doing; otherwise, the name describes what you'll look like if you rip your gear.

39. **The Go Between** (5.11+) ★ Just right of *Jam and Jelly*. Start in the crack or use the optional face start just to the right (B1). Up over the roof to the anchors. FA: Mike Dahlberg.

Near the top of *Jam and Jelly* a large ledge runs out to the right. The next three routes end just below this ledge and share a common start below a 3-inch pocket about 15 feet up. This pocket is directly above the highest point of ground right of Jam and Jelly.

40. **Foreign Affairs** (5.10d/11a) ★★ Start up *Chinese Freedom* and diverge left to the anchors near the top of *Jam and Jelly*. Several optional boulder starts are found to the left. FA: Mike Dahlberg.

41. **Chinese Freedom** (5.11d) ★★★ A technical crux, two hueco jugs, and a steep finish will test your mettle. Up to the hueco and straight up to a two-carabiner anchor near the center of the ledge above. FA: Nate Postma.

42. **Do the Right Thing** (5.12a) ★ This route takes the right-hand finish above the start of *Chinese Freedom*, ending just left of an inside corner. FA: Mike Dahlberg.

43. **Paradigm Shift** (5.12d) ★★★ Just left of *Barnburner* are three lines of bolts. This is the left line. FA: Mike Dahlberg.

44. **Project** (5.?) Start on the previous route, move right and up. Bolted by Rich Aschert.

45. **Mississippi Burning** (5.12c) ★★★ A chip off the old block? The right-hand line. For full value, avoid resting on *Barnburner*. FA: Keith Anderson.

46. **Barnburner** (5.10d) ★★★ At the right end of The Winter Wall is an obvious, thin crack. This has been led many times with gear, and retrobolting gives sport climbing a bad name. The right hand finish (up the face) is 5.11c. FA: Jim Blakley.

Where protection is not assured by a usable crack, long unprotected
runouts sometimes result, and the leader of commitment must
be prepared to accept the risks and alternatives which are only too
well defined. Personal qualities—judgment, concentration, boldness—
the ordeal by fire, take precedence, as they should, over mere
hardware . . . But every climb is not for every climber;
the ultimate climbs are not democratic.

—DOUG ROBINSON

47. **Living All over Me** (5.12b) ★★★ Just right of *Barnburner*. Hard, technical, short. A Tom Deuchler top-rope exists in the same area. FA: Tom Ramier.

THE EAST END

As you proceed right of *Barnburner*, you round the corner past a six-foot-wide buttress (*The Prow*). The twenty-foot face to the right of that buttress ends in a left-facing dihedral (*Barnie's Corner*). The next 8 routes are not pictured.

48. **The Prow** (5.8) Top-rope on the buttress.

49. **Dead Dog Arete** (5.10) Top-rope on the buttress.

50. **Dead Dog Face** (5.11a) ★★ This route takes the bolted face between a pedestal and the major roof 15' up.

51. **Barn Dance** (5.9) ★★ Top-rope or use bolts on *Dead Dog Face*. Up to the corner left of the roof.

52. **Roof Burner** (5.11) ★★★ Two roofs and a bulge crux make for some kind of fun. Jet directly over the major roof to the right of *Dead Dog Face*. FA: Nate Postma, 1991.

53. **Barnie's Corner** (5.9+) Top-rope or lead to protect it adequately.

54. **Thief of Wives** (V7) ★★ On the dark right wall of *Barnie's Corner* is a hard boulder problem. Use only the face on the lower part; the arete is on route after the tiny triangular roof. FA: Jeremy Mariette.

55. **Left Lane** (5.10a) ★★ Start on the flat face of the buttress, up white rock, keeping left of the round nose above. FA: Nate Postma, 1991.

56. **Sunburst** (5.7-) ★★ On the face of the buttress, just right of *Left Lane*, find a bolt about 8' up on gray rock. Stay just right of the rounded nose above. FA: Nate Postma, 1991.

ANNADONIA AREA

This area begins at the right side of the protruding gray Sunburst Buttress. The next few routes lie on the Generic Wall, which contains several similar routes. Rocks are often thrown off the top in this area; I've seen several close calls.

57. **Cardiac Standstill** (5.9+) ★★ This may happen if you stray from the most parsimonious route. On the right side of the *Sunburst* buttress is a shallow, inside corner with a 6-foot block as its base. Stay several feet left of this dihedral and weave up to some chains. Stay right at the third bolt for a 5.10b.

58. **Freebase** (5.9-) Lead or top-rope this corner/crack.

59. **Rock-a-holics** (5.8) ★ Eight feet right of *Freebase* and just left of a little buttress. FA: Nate Postma, 1991.

60. **Danger High Boltage** (5.9-) ★ Locate a juniper near the top. Start on ledges a few feet left of the tree (at a thin crack) and move right, up, and back left to the top.

61. **Too Low For Zero** (5.8+) ★ This route and the next start to the right of Route 60, before the face curves toward *Cookie Crumble*. Start up a face leading to a 6-inch ledge at 12'.

GENERIC WALL—LEFT

GENERIC WALL—RIGHT

ANNADONIA AREA

62. **Year of the Ankle** (5.9) ★ Just left of the right edge of the face. FA: Nate Postma, 1992.

63. **Micro Balls** (5.9+) ★★ About 10' right of the previous route, around the corner. FA: Dan Meyer.

64. **Cinq Jour D'Affille** (5.7) ★ Eight feet left of *Cookie Crumble*. FA: Nate Postma and Penny Sperlak, 1991.

65. **Cookie Crumble** (5.9) The obvious corner that you should obviously avoid climbing.

66. **ESP** (5.11d) Four feet right of *Cookie Crumble* is a line of bolts. Start from the platform.

67. **Femme Fatale** (5.12c) ★★★ Start on the block at the base of *ESP* and move up and right. A direct start takes the bolts just right of the pedestal. FA: Nate Postma, 1991.

68. **Quiet Desperation** (5.12d) ★★ Six feet right of *ESP*, work up the arete. FA: Jeff Engel.

69. **Campinini** (5.12a) ★★ This route goes up the left wall of the shallow dihedral of Route 70. FA: Tom Ramier.

70. **Geriatric Sex Maniacs from Mars** (5.10c) ★★ Right of the *Cookie Crumble* corner is a sloping ledge about 25' up. Below and right of the ledge is a shallow corner. Above the ledge is a shallow dihedral. Climb from the corner to the ledge and up the dihedral. FA: Nate Postma, 1989.

71. **Out of Control** (5.11a) ★★ From the ledge of the previous route, forge up a line of bolts that ends about 6' right of Route 70's finish. Steep huecos at the top provide the crux. FA: Nate Postma, 1989.

72. **Stylin'** (5.11a) ★ This route leads from the aforementioned ledge to a finish about 6' right of *Out of Control*. Whimper across some thin horizontal face moves to overhanging jugs. FA: Nate Postma, 1989. You may also be able to top-rope a direct start.

73. **Annadonia** (5.11b) ★★★ About 12 feet right of the Route 70 ledge is a thin crack that peters out before it reaches the ground. A bouldery start leads to excellent climbing and another crux at the top. There is a 5.12a finish to the right, up the steep nose. FA: Nate Postma, 1989.

74. **Looking for Lust** (5.9-) ★★★ You may be looking for thrust. Long and varied with a loose finish, it starts as a right-leaning lieback flake 8' right of *Annadonia*. Nine bolts. FA: Nate Postma, 1989.

75. **Dirty Corner** (5.9?) Why?

From the large gray buttress (right of *Looking for Lust*) to the scree pile 75' west is an area in which owls roost. Climbing is prohibited here from February to June.

76. **Cool for Cats** (5.10) ★ Start on the right side of the buttress right of *Looking for Lust*. Climb up to the chains below the first grassy ledge. FA: Jeff Engel.

77. **Vertical Willies** (5.11) A top-rope problem right of the previous route.

78. **Rude Awakening** (5.11b) ★ Moving past the Annadonia Area you will pass a talus area with some TV-sized blocks (the right end of the owl closure). Immediately right of the talus is a line of six bolts 20' right of a grungy, hanging gully. FA: Kelly Gorder and Scott Wright.

79. **Last Call for Alcohol** (5.10a) ★★ Thirty feet right of the previous route, just right of a very straight tree next to the wall. FA: Kelly Gorder and Scott Wright.

PERFECT CRIMB AREA

Go past *Looking for Lust* and follow the trail between some large boulders on a dirt slope. These allow access to the top and mark the beginning of the *Perfect Crimb* area, which ends at the quarry bolt buttress about 90 yards to the west. The routes are located at a set of roofs about 170 feet west of the summit access boulders.

80. **One Hand Jam** (5.6) Two corners left of *Perfect Crimb* is a bolted crack/face. FA: Jeff Engel.

81. **Don't Mean Nothin'** (5.10b) ★ A good trad lead for the qualified climber; the face left of *Technical Difficulties* has a thin crack leading to a lowering station. FA: Nate Postma, 1990.

82. **Technical Difficulties** (5.12c) ★ The outside corner to the left of *Perfect Crimb*; hug the whale to the top. FA: Mike Dahlberg.

83. **Vice Squad** (5.12d) ★ Just left of *Perfect Crimb* is this crimpfest. FA: Mike Dahlberg.

84. **Perfect Crimb** (5.9) ★★★ Except for some dirt and a possible loose block near the top, a good route. A thin crack runs down from the left edge of the main roof to a small pedestal at the base. Crimb up the obvious shallow dihedral just left of the large roof. FA: Nate Postma, 1990.

85. **Pulldown Menu** (5.12d) ★★ Just right of *Perfect Crimb*, climb up to the left side of the main roof. Move right to the chains. FA: Mike Dahlberg.

86. **Fallout, a.k.a. Perfect Sex** (5.12b) ★ The crux has been described as "a biped surf move to a jacked stance." Follow the line on the photo. FTR: Nate Postma, 1990. FL: Mike Dahlberg.

87. **Advanced Birding** (5.12b) ★★★ The first ascent was delayed until the baby birds left the nest. What's left is crimpy face climbing, in contrast to the power routes to the left. FA: Mike Dahlberg.

88. **Hateful Pleasures** (5.9) ★ Start up the bolts at the right edge of the main roof, then switch to nuts. FA: Mike Dahlberg.

89. **Gear Fear** (5.10a) ★ There is a thin crack just right of *Hateful Pleasures*. Use the lower bolts of *Crank-n-Go-Go*, then tremble up the left crack. Take nuts, obviously. FA: Mike Dahlberg.

PERFECT CRIMB—LEFT

PERFECT CRIMB—RIGHT

90. **Crank-n-Go-Go** (5.10d) ★★ The blunt arete right of *Gear Fear*; 5.11b direct start. FA: Jeff Engel.

91. **Lacuna** (5.12b/c) Right of *Crank-n-Go-Go* about 25'. Scrabble up a dirt ramp to the base of a chimney-like structure to the first bolt. Watch for a scary finish. FA: Mike Dahlberg.

NEW VICE AREA

The left (east) end of this area starts at a large eyebolt on a buttress that forms the wall of a large, right-facing corner and ends about 120 yards to the west at a dirt and scree pile.

92. **Eye Bolt Approach** (5.4) Right of the eyebolt is either an easy top-rope or an approach route.

93. **Unknown** (5.7) It is unclear if this route is distinct from the next one.

94. **Jenna's Chimney** (5.5) As you go around the corner from the quarry eyebolt there is a large, right-facing corner (*Jenna's Chimney*) with a compact gray wall to the right. A tree leans across to the quarry bolt buttress. Two or more bolts left of the crack lead to chains at top of chimney

95. **Jenna's Face** (5.8) ★ This route starts as a crack and flake about 10' right of the corner. Placing a stopper near the bottom is a good idea. The top can be mossy and wet.

96. **New Tomorrow** (5.12a) Variable reports on this route. Find a line of bolts about 6' right of previous route. Unique rock, but the bolts are not the best. FA: Nate Postma, 1989.

97. **Eggs and Darts and Shit** (5.12b) Twelve feet right of *New Tomorrow* is a line of bolts. Start up the ramp. FA: Nate Postma and Brett Harberts, 1992.

98. **Way Knarly Dudes** (5.8) Right of *Eggs* . . . is an ugly pedestal that forms two dihedrals. This is the left-hand corner. FA: Nate Postma, 1991.

99. **Syncopation** (5.8) This is the right-hand corner.

100. **B.F. Bugs** (5.9+) ★ Just right of *Syncopation* is a face for you to climb. FA: Nate Postma, 1991.

101. **Pleasant Summer Absence** (5.10a) ★ This four-bolt line is just right of a tiny, right-facing flake-corner. It starts a few steps right of the previous route. FA: Nate Postma, 1991.

102. **Pandemonium** (5.10a) ★ Just left of *Vertical Vice*. FA: Nate Postma and Brett Harberts, 1992.

103. **Vertical Vice** (5.8+) ★★ About 15' left of *Goofed on Skunkweed* is a short arete (black on the right, white on the left). Start up the left side of this arete and weave your way up to the chains under the rectangular roof above. Very, very slick after all the traffic. FTR: Mike Dahlberg and Melissa Quigley; FL: Nate Postma and Steve Wilgge, 1989 (bolted on lead).

104. **Three Fat Chicks on a World Tour** (5.11b) ★ Essentially a variation on the next route. Start on the face left of *Call of the Mild* and climb up the face, joining the next route above its corner. FA: Nate Postma and Dan Meyer, 1989.

105. **Call of the Mild** (5.11b) ★ Right of *Vertical Vice* is a short dihedral. The route goes up this corner (thread a sling up higher in the drill hole) and follows a slight arete (bolted) above. FA: Mike Dahlberg.

106. **Goofed on Skunkweed** (5.8-) ★★ Climb the finger- and hand-sized crack, which also accommodates flying mammals very nicely. Good trad lead. Check the top anchors and don't top-rope by laying the rope over the hooks. FA: Nate Postma, 1990.

107. **Alligator Alimony** (5.7+) Arete, top-rope from next route. FA: Nate Postma, 1990.

108. **Two Tone Zephyr** (5.9) ★★★ There is a flat, gray face around the corner to the right from the previous route. On the left edge of the face is a crack. Climb up the face to the crack, and then to a tiny left-facing dihedral. The hangers are dangerous and need to be replaced. FA: Nate Postma and Jeff Engel, 1990.

109. **Eel Pocket Route** (5.10b) ★ Top-rope, 3' left of *Doctor Limit*. Look for pocket that might conceal an eel. FA: Nate Postma, 1990.

110. **Doctor Limit** (5.11b/c) ★★ The next line of bolts to the right of *Two Tone Zephyr* and 6' left of *Frequent Flatulence*. This route is very hard to lead on sight due to blind reaches to hidden holds. Look forward to a delicate leftward traverse and strenuous fingertip cranks.

NEW VICE
AREA—LEFT

NEW VICE AREA—RIGHT

111. **Frequent Flatulence** (5.10b) ★★★ In the middle of this face is a thin crack meandering up and right. Start at the left edge of the ledge, then head straight up the thin crack. More scary hangers need to be fixed. FA: Nate Postma, 1990.

112. **Doctor Rock** (5.10c) ★ Start at the right end of the *Frequent Flatulence* ledge and directly below a small overhang. Climb straight up. Those of you with a only a bachelor's degree might swing to the right above the roof for a slightly easier version. FA: Nate Postma, 1990.

113. **Living Postmortems** (5.8-) ★ Some bolts, but you need pro, too (big). Enjoy the moveable flake. FA: Nate Postma, 1991.

114. **No Whippin Boys** (5.10a) ★★★ A rarity at the bluff—a nice finger crack. Just right of a black, right-facing dihedral is a crack leading to a multi-stemmed birch. FA: Nate Postma, 1989.

115. **Prairie Fire** (5.10c) ★★★ Start 15' right of the crack, move up and right to first bolt, straight up to second, then trend left to chains on *No Whippin Boys*. FA: Dave Brant, 1996.

116. **Dealer's Choice** (5.6) Farther right find a gully with chains. A direct start is possible (5.11b). FA: Jim Blakely (gully); Dave Brandt (direct start), 1996.

117. **Blue Moon** (5.10) ★★ At the top of the dirt pile and just right of a small prow is a nice short climb. FA: Jim Craighead, 1996.

LARGE ROOF AREA

This area starts right of the dirt/scree pile and ends at the large roof 50 yards west.

118. **In the Pink** (5.11a) ★ Thirty feet right of the scree is a talus block that marks the start of the next three routes. Find three lines of bolts, the middle one starting at the top of a pancake flake. This is the left line. FA: Nate Postma, 1990.

119. **Quick Draw Moves to Hollywood** (5.11b) ★★★ The middle line. Watch the groundfall potential on a tough clip. Three cold shuts at the top. FA: Jeff Engel.

120. **Space Warp** (5.11d) The right-hand line. FA: Nate Postma, 1990.

121. **Why Doesn't Anybody Climb This** (5.10a) Just right of a line of saplings in a faint corner/seam. All the routes over to *Toll Free* are dirty and almost never done. FA: Nate Postma, 1992.

122. **Tub Toys** (5.10a) A hueco at the first bolt, 12' right of Route 121. FA: Nate Postma 1992.

123. **Fish Furniture** (5.11a) The next route on the grid, 6' right of Route 122; 5 bolts. FA: Nate Postma 1991.

LARGE ROOF AREA—LEFT

124. **Multiple Stab Wounds** (5.11a) ★ The next route on the grid, 7' right of Route 123; 4 bolts. FA: Nate Postma, 1991.

125. **Toll Free** (5.9+) Top-rope from the next route. FA: Nate Postma, 1991.

126. **Needles and Pins** (5.10a) ★★★ Fifteen feet left of the triangular overhang is a blunt arete on a black wall with a small roof below the first bolt. Climb up to the pocket, pass some small roofs on the right, then try to figure out the last moves. FA: Nate Postma, 1989.

127. **Dances with Pete** (5.11d) ★★ Just right of *Needles and Pins* is this one-move wonder. FA: Nate Postma and Pete Olson, 1991.

128. **A Deal with the Devil** (5.10c) ★ Is it worth it for a measly 5.10? Use long runners for rope drag as you turn the roof on the left. There are a couple of stray bolts under the roof. FA: Nate Postma, 1990.

129. **Talking with God** (5.11d) ★★★ Ask her for another 6 inches in height to help you pull the roof. There is a secret foot pocket and head jam below the roof. Up the corner to the notch in the right side the roof, then pull it. FA: Nate Postma, 1990.

130. **Weenies and Nerds** (5.10d) ★★★ Up the corner (see above for secret rest), go right under the roof, around the corner, then fake left to the Route 129 anchors. FA: Nate Postma, 1990.

131. **Climb or Die** (5.12c) ★★ Straight up through small roofs to the larger roof at the top. FTR: Nate Postma, 1992; FL: Jeremy Mariette, 1999.

132. **Arachnid Tendencies** (5.11d) ★★ Right of the large roof is a flat face of yellow rock. Start about two feet left of the right edge of this face, near a thin crack. A sporty start, improbable stemming, and some loose rock may test your exoskeleton. *Arachnophobia*, a direct finish, goes straight up after bolt 5 or 6 (5.12-?). FA: Jeff Engel.

133. **Dumpster Does Duffels** (5.10b) ★ This may be 5.10d for shorter folks. A tricky mantle halfway up is one of the technical tests on this route. Climb the black face around the corner to the right of *Arachnid Tendencies*, generally following a thin seam. FA: Nate Postma.

WILLOW RIVER OVERVIEW

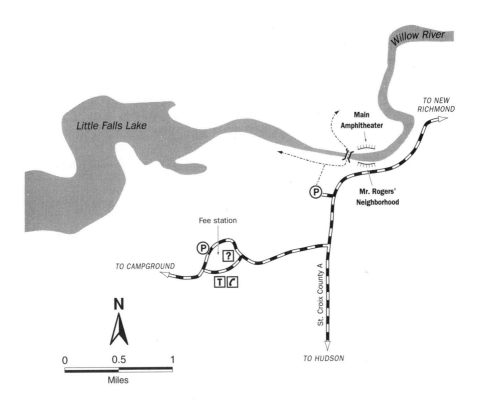

Willow River

Little Falls Lake

TO NEW RICHMOND

Main Amphitheater

Mr. Rogers' Neighborhood

Fee station

TO CAMPGROUND

St. Croix County A

TO HUDSON

N

0   0.5   1

Miles

WILLOW RIVER

You'd better be good and strong. This is not the place to come and play around—it's an area for advanced climbers to try some of the steepest ground in the Midwest. Climbing access is in flux here, and continued use of the area will depend on our being sensitive to the concerns of the land managers. If you see climbers endangering access here in some way, please intervene immediately; self regulation is much preferable to closing the area. Go lead all of the roof routes at Red Wing and you'll be ready to climb here.

Emergency contact: Dial 911. The park office number is 715-386-5931. The nearest hospital is the Hudson Medical Center at 400 Wisconsin Street in Hudson, WI (715-386-9321).

The climbing environment: The rock is the same dolomite found at Barn Bluff in Red Wing and is reasonably solid after the routes have been cleaned. The routes are bolted; take along plenty of quickdraws as well as a painted lower-off biner. No star ratings are given due to the changing nature of the climbs and the relatively few ascents of most routes to date.

Register at the Visitor Center at the beginning of the climbing season, and pay entry fees every time you climb (or buy an annual pass). Check with park officials every month or so to make sure that you are up on the most recent changes in access policy. Route development is restricted and you must consult with park officials before contemplating new routes.

Currently, climbing is only allowed during certain times on certain days. The schedule is subject to change and should be verified before climbing. After Labor Day weekend and before Memorial Day weekend you can climb anytime the park is open. From Memorial Day weekend to Labor Day weekend (including those weekends) climbing is permitted all day Monday–Thursday, until noon on Friday and Sunday, and no climbing is permitted on Saturdays. Please maintain a low profile to avoid complaints from non-climbers. The river is very noisy, so arrange hand signals with your belayer to avoid useless shouting.

Future access at Willow River depends on limiting the ecological and visual impacts of climbers. This means: very minimal chalk (not a big deal, given the big holds); no fixed quickdraws—retreat via a brown-painted carabiner, as anything else will be removed; absolutely no rappelling from the top.

Projects are marked with a string tied to the first bolt. These routes may not be cleaned or completely bolted. For your safety and out of respect to the route developer, leave the projects alone. It is imperative that you consult with those who have developed the routes here before you attempt to develop a new route; the park office will be able to provide you with contact information.

Services: The freeway interchanges, Hudson, and the Twin Cities provide increasingly higher levels of service. The Twin Cities area offers a number of climbing shops. Midwest Mountaineering, Vertical Endeavors, and P.J. Asch Otterfitters are locally owned. Chain stores include REI (Bloomington and Roseville) and Eastern Mountain Sports (Burnsville). See Appendix A for more information.

Approach: From the south, east , or west, take Interstate 94 to the U.S. Highway 12 exit, 4 miles east of the Minnesota border. Go north on US 12, following signs for Willow River State Park. Turn left on St. Croix County Road U (not on UU) after 1.8 miles. This morphs into St. Croix County Road A and you reach the main entrance in another 2 miles. Turn in here to register if necessary and pay entry fees. Go back out to the main road and drive 0.3 mile north to a paved parking lot. There is also a self-service fee station in this lot.

From the back of the lot, follow the gravel road for 50 yards, then turn left on the wide trail leading downhill to the bottom of the bluff. Turn right along the river for a couple of minutes to the bridge and the climbing area.

MAIN AMPHITHEATER

After crossing the river on the footbridge take an immediate right. Walk along the base of the small 10-foot cliff for about 120 feet to two small caves. Between them is a tree about a foot from the base of the cliff. Boulder up the cliff at this point, or continue along the base of the cliff until there is no cliff. You must hop across one or more small offshoots of the main river in a couple of places if you go this way.

1. **Jars of Flys** (5.9) Start just right of a small prow a few feet up. Climb slab to the left of large horizontal roof to chains located to the left of the crack. FA: Josh Helke and Jeff Engel. Not recommended.

2. **White Noise** (5.10d/5.11a) Start on a small platform just beneath the overhang at the base and climb slightly overhanging rock up to and over the right side of a large horizontal roof to the left set of anchors. FA: Todd Peterson.

3. **Daily Grind** (5.11a) Start on a corner above pointed and flat talus blocks. Climb slightly overhanging rock that passes just right of a large horizontal roof. FA: Paul Bjork.

4. **Sudden Shock** (5.11d) Start at large pockets in a blackened area, just left of a brown block. Climb up the left side of the large black streak. End just right of a drooping juniper. FA: Jeff Engel.

MAIN CAVE—LEFT

5. **Midsummer Daydreams** (5.13a) Directly behind a two-pronged talus block, follow a small arete up to overhanging rock. Climb overhanging rock just to right of a black streak. FA: Jeff Engel.

6. **Natural Selection** (5.12b/c) Start 6' right of Route 5, right of a shallow corner. Climb the slab to the 45-degree overhanging rock with large pockets. Follow large pockets up and left to a small horizontal roof. Flop over the roof and continue up less overhanging rock to the top. FA: Jeff Engel.

7. **Tsunami** (5.13a/b) Go right at 4th bolt on *Natural Selection*.

8. **Genesis Effect** (5.12d) Three feet left of the black cave at the base, climb the slab to the 45-degree overhang. Follow bolts up and right to the top. FA: Jeff Engel and Paul Bjork.

9. **Big Kahuna—direct (project)** Start just left of a roof crack and go out the blank 6-foot horizontal roof to meet up with *Big Kahuna*.

10. **Big Kahuna (project)** Go left after getting to lip on crack in the 12-foot roof.

11. **Project** Go straight up after getting to lip on crack in the 12-foot roof.

12. **Rejection and Mercy** (5.13a) Find a corner with two large blocks at the base. Climb the crack through a 12-foot horizontal roof. At the lip follow bolts up and right to top. FA: Paul Bjork.

13. **Water Music** (5.12a) Starts just left of where the rock gets wet from the falls, just right of an 8-foot, shallow black inset. Go up and left to chains halfway up the main amphitheater, just below a large horizontal roof. FA: Mike Dahlberg.

14. **Project** Climb on left side of prominent arete on far right side of amphitheater.

15. **Project** Middle of steep rock above falls.

16. **Doppler Effect** (5.12a) Climb dead-vertical face on right side of rock above the falls. Stick-clip the first bolt. There is a belay bolt on the ledge. FA: Josh Helke.

MISTER ROGERS' NEIGHBORHOOD

These routes are on the south side of the river. The routes are described as "always changing, but nice when dry." Do not remove the moss gardens between Routes 18, 19, and 20, and do not bolt in those areas. Some of the slimy rock on the approach has absolutely no friction underfoot. These routes are not pictured.

17. **Pride and Prejudice** (5.12a) Start about 30' right of the pipe, behind two blocks. Stick-clip the second bolt and climb loose rock to good rock above. FA: Josh Helke.

18. **Speedy Delivery** (5.12a) Start at a white pedestal just right of *Pride and Prejudice*. FA: Josh Helke.

19. **Project** Left of *Double Trouble*.

20. **Double Trouble** (5.11) On the right side of the black amphitheater. There is a hanging belay off the ledge. Stick-clip the first bolt and dance up loose rock. FA: Josh Helke.

"The upper rim was fanged in black, and black rock gleamed hungrily at us through a thousand green and dripping moustachios . . . The cress hiccuped vertiginously. I grabbed several stems, pressed kneecaps into a Gorgon's head of bryophytes. The Apprentice said he was getting the hell out of here and boldly struck off leftward into a succession of roofs, mere vertical or overhanging rock relatively free of photosynthetic organisms and their less ambitious brethren . . ."

—G.J.F. Dutton, *The Craggie*

Stephen Regenold on #6 (The Bulge). PHOTO BY BEN REGENOLD

TAYLORS FALLS

I was damn glad I was with George [Lowe]. He was solid. I told him of
my confidence, and he replied that he felt the same way. I might be
lousy on 5.10, but he reckoned I had a high survival potential.

—CHRIS JONES, *North Twin, North Face*

Taylors Falls is reminiscent of Yosemite Valley—not because of the type of rock
or quality of climbing, but because of the close association between large masses
of humanity and a unique geological system. One can drive almost to the foot
of the Minnesota crags, and the hiking approaches are short and easy on both
sides of the river. This is probably the most visited climbing spot in Minnesota
due to its proximity to the Twin Cities, the easy access, and solid rock. The
cliffs rise above the St. Croix, a nationally designated Wild and Scenic River.
The river also forms the border between Minnesota and Wisconsin.

Europeans started to exploit this area in the 1830s. Earlier, the St. Croix
was named by Sieur du Lhut upon seeing the cross in the rocks on the Wisconsin side of The Dalles. The great white pine forests of northern Minnesota ex-
tended south to the Taylors Falls area. Virtually all of these trees were cut and
floated down the St. Croix to provide most of the construction lumber used in
the United States between 1860 and 1890. Huge logjams were common in the
narrowest part of The Dalles; pictures of these can be seen in the interpretive
center on the Minnesota side. Similar logjams can be seen in the autumn along
U.S. Highway 8 as people flock to look at the colorful leaves, and on the climbs
along the main strips on the first nice weekends of spring.

Emergency Contact: Minnesota: Call 911 or the Minnesota Park Office at
612-465-5711. Wisconsin: Call 911 or the Wisconsin Park Office at 715-483-
3747. On the Wisconsin side, public phones are located at the entrance station
and at the building on the left as you descend the big curve. The nearest phone
in Minnesota is at the gas station across U.S. Highway 8. Report all accidents
to the proper park office.

The climbing environment: This climbing area is split between two states
(and two state parks). On weekdays, an entrance pass for one state allows entry
to the other side as well. On weekends, entrance fees must be paid separately.
The Wisconsin park honors federal Golden Eagle passes at all times, and these
passes are available at the Wild and Scenic River office in downtown St. Croix
Falls, Wisconsin. The parks are connected for pedestrians by the US 8 bridge

TAYLORS FALLS OVERVIEW

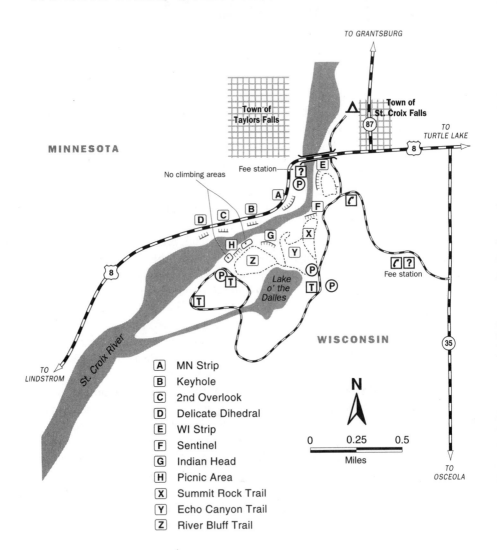

TO GRANTSBURG

Town of
Taylors Falls

Town of
St. Croix Falls

87

TO
TURTLE LAKE

MINNESOTA

8

Fee station

No climbing areas

? E

P

A

D C B

F

G X

H

Z Y

P T

P

T

T P

Lake
o' the
Dalles

Fee station

?

WISCONSIN

8

35

TO
LINDSTROM

St. Croix River

A	MN Strip
B	Keyhole
C	2nd Overlook
D	Delicate Dihedral
E	WI Strip
F	Sentinel
G	Indian Head
H	Picnic Area
X	Summit Rock Trail
Y	Echo Canyon Trail
Z	River Bluff Trail

N

0   0.25   0.5

Miles

TO
OSCEOLA

walkway. Both parks have interpretive centers, and the Minnesota park has a bookstore near the riverboat parking lot. Campgrounds are available in both parks, although they may be very busy or full on the weekends. Private campgrounds are also found in the area.

The Minnesota and Wisconsin units of the park offer somewhat different environments for the climber. The Minnesota side is much smaller and the approaches are shorter. The Wisconsin park conducts more patrols with officers who are well known for their no-nonsense approach.

The biggest hurdle in writing this section has been deciding on the "correct" names for climbs. There have been three previous guides for this area: Swenson, Roberts, and Schmidt published *The Climber's Guide to Taylors Falls* in 1972. Peter VonGrossman and Peter Scott published *Close to the Edge, Down by the River* in 1988. I published a selection of routes in *Minnesota Rock: Selected Climbs* in 1995. The first guide had only a fraction of the routes presented here, and the latter two guides both applied new names that usurped the older names for some climbs. In this guide, I have tried to determine the original names of routes. Once found, I had to decide what to do with them. In some cases (e.g., *Double Cracks*), I restored the original name. In other cases (e.g., *Batman*) I felt that restoring the original name was too problematic. I have included many of the alternative names so we'll all know which route I'm referring to. There are actually few changes, and I hope these editorial decisions don't trouble you too much. I'm certain that there are still historically incorrect names listed in this guide.

The basalt is generally sound, although a lot of people have been bopped by loose stuff while climbing or belaying. Those big blocks that some think are good top-rope anchors have a habit of falling off, so use the many good nut placements available. Watch for glass on the approach gully just past *The Bulge* and on most outcrops on the Wisconsin side.

Wasps have become more numerous in recent years, and many climbs become unpleasant (but not dangerous) to attempt at certain times of the year as a result. They seldom attack unless provoked, but that is easy to do since they often occupy handholds and lurk just inside those nice horizontal cracks. Their activity is directly proportional to the temperature, so warm days present the most excitement. If you are allergic, carry appropriate medication. My experience is that they tend to be more aggressive in the autumn.

The Minnesota Climbing Management Plan: *Climber Registration*—Rock climbing permits will be valid for the calendar year and may be obtained free of charge, in person or by mail, by contacting the park office.

Closures—Rock climbing is generally allowed within the "Dalles" area of Interstate State Park as described in this guide. Climbing will not be permitted in or on any glacial pothole, the Devil's Chair, or any area posted as closed to climbing.

New route development within this area is allowed within this policy without further permission as long as no additional fixed anchors are required. Climbers who wish to climb or develop new routes outside of these areas or in other parts of the park may request permission in writing through the park manager. Requests for new routes will be reviewed to determine the appropriateness of the request and the impact on park resources.

Alteration of the Natural Environment—The local climbing ethic at Interstate State Park has been the acceptance of white chalk. Use of white chalk will be allowed with a voluntary reduction of its use encouraged. Information on alternative products will be made available to climbers.

Wisconsin Climbing Management Plan: The Wisconsin cliffs are part of the Ice Age National Scientific Reserve as well as the state park. This designation gives managers more latitude in dealing with perceived problems. In Wisconsin there are areas that are closed to climbing and hiking due to erosion damage in the access gullies (caused by both climbers and tourists). This includes climbs such as *Unseemly* and *The Cross*. The climbs in these areas are not described in this book; please respect these and other closures (or face a $90 fine). Absolutely no pitons or bolts may be placed. Trees may be used as anchors, but slings may not obstruct trails.

Wisconsin park officials have been very concerned about food and beverages in the bluff area. Be discrete with your food and consider taking a trash bag along and picking up any debris you find. Finally, bicycling is not allowed on trails. Those climbers who store their bikes in the pothole above the Wisconsin Strip only make access issues more difficult to resolve.

Services: Both Taylors Falls, Minnesota, and St. Croix Falls, Wisconsin, have most services, unless you need climbing gear. The Border Bar is highly recommended for after-climb burgers. Spend a few minutes in the interpretive centers on both sides of the river and learn about the biology and history of this area.

The Twin Cities area offers a number of climbing shops. Midwest Mountaineering, Vertical Endeavors, and P.J. Asch Otterfitters are locally owned. Chain stores include REI (Bloomington and Roseville) and Eastern Mountain Sports (Burnsville). See Appendix A for more information.

Approach: The river provides a natural landmark for locating the climbs. Routes are generally described from north (upriver) to south. I will use north and south to indicate directions, though the cliffs may face somewhat different ways.

MINNESOTA

You share the cliff tops and bottoms with a cross section of society, although the closure of the main overlook on U.S. Highway 8 has made things more pleasant for climbers. In return, you have a chance to try a wide range of high quality climbs from 5.4 to 5.13 and to meet a lot of other climbers.

The access to all of these routes begins from the State Park parking lot, which is just south and west of the US 8 bridge (a stoplight marks the intersection). Parking is no longer allowed along US 8 above the climbs. From the parking lot, a paved access road runs downhill from the locked gate at the south end of the lot to the lower riverboat dock. At this boat dock, a trail briefly follows the river, then heads up over talus to the obvious cliffband known as The Minnesota Strip. Most people seem to end up below the start of *Piece of Cake*. By staying low along the river, the base of Devil's Chair (closed to climbing) is reached just beyond The Minnesota Strip. To reach the Keyhole area and areas downstream you must hike along the highway as described later.

TAYLORS FALLS, MINNESOTA
PARKING AREA DETAIL

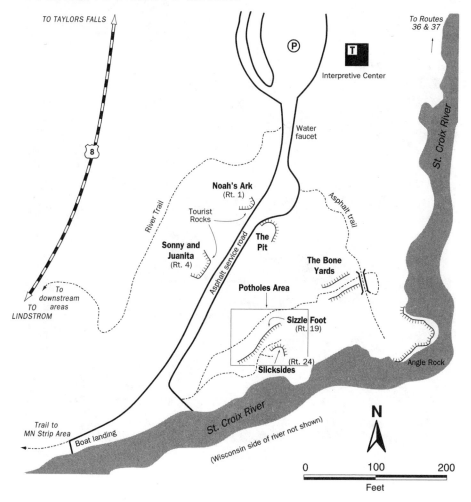

VAR.

1

VAR.

NOAH'S ARK

TOURIST ROCKS

These outcrops are located along the paved road leading south from the parking lot. Noah's Ark is the small outcrop with some reddish rock at the base, located across the road from the first railing, which is above The Pit. The Sonny and Juanita Area is 30 yards farther down the road on the same side as Noah's Ark and is marked by the large gravel patch at its base.

1. **Noah's Ark** (5.6) ★★ Be prepared for a flood of people walking by. Start just right of the slab rising to the left. Surmounting the crux first moves allows you to zig right up the tiny ramp. Zag left along good handholds to exit left of the prow. For a 5.8 variation, fire straight up the little dihedral 15 inches left of the regular start, or stay around the corner right of the regular start (5.8+).

There is some junky rock between *Noah's Ark* and the *Sonny and Juanita* area, none of which is worth the effort of setting up a rope.

2. **Gorilla Killer** (5.10a-c) ★ To the right of *Sonny and Juanita* is an arete capped by an overhang. Climb up the arete, then monkey around looking for a route through the roof—the more direct, the harder the climb.

3. **Daphnis and Chloe** (5.8) ★ Climb up just right of *Sonny and Juanita*, smugly avoiding the dihedral, ledge, etc.

4. **Sonny and Juanita** (5.5) ★★★ Pick a number and be prepared for an audience. Any difficulty you encounter stems from a lack of technique. Surmount the right-facing dihedral to a ledge and pull through overhanging blocks to the belay tree. You can actually do this as three pitches. Two of

the more interesting variations are a contrived 5.10 lieback a few inches left of the main corner and a hard finish up the smooth, steep wall left of the final crack.

5. **Bill and Tom** (5.7) ★ Start up Route 4, cut up and left along the flake on the left wall to join *The Cornice*, or start to the right of *The Cornice* (5.9), or go straight up the middle of the face (5.hard).

6. **The Cornice** (5.6) ★★ Ancient laws require that you don't touch the tree. Of course, the tree used to be smaller (as did the rating). Various starts lead up to and right of the tree, then finish up a little dihedral and crack just left of the arete.

7. **The Other One** (5.5) ★★★ A good climb for the beginner. Balance up the first wall, surmount a block, and cruise to the top. There are several moderate variations on the lower wall, and a rather strenuous mantle up the face of the block.

There is more junky rock down by the boat landing that deserves to be ignored.

THE PIT
Several routes are found in the little pit (creatively named "The Pit") just across the road from Noah's Ark. Spot the triangular overhang with a tree at the top. Please don't use this tree as an anchor.

8. **Armpit** (5.8+) ★★ Straight up this face without using any of the obvious holds on the right or the left.

9. **Dihedral** (5.3) Now you can use the easy corner to the right.

10. **The Overhang** (5.6) ★★ Up the left corner of the face beneath the triangular overhang. Go left of the overhang, and you must top out to claim an ascent.

11. **The Overhang Face** (5.9) ★★ Avoid both corners.

12. **Corner Staircase** (4th) A great kid's climb.

13. **One Thin Fish** (5.9+) Stay left of the crack until you get to the very top. Don't use the ledge. The rating is traditional.

14. **The Crack** (5.9-) ★ It's the crack.

15. **Boob** (5.7) On the corner.

POTHOLES AREA

These routes are quite short but most are easily approached. Most climbs lie between the paved road and the river (see the area map on page 153). They are generally described south to north (towards the bridge). No climbing is allowed in the potholes that are part of the interpretive trail, or those that are filled with water. Regulations prohibit the use of artificial structures (such as railings) as anchors, making some routes more difficult to top-rope.

There are many, many boulder problems in this area. To learn about them, find the wizened old man who emerges from the deepest pothole only on a full moon . . . or follow the chalk.

POTHOLES—
SIZZLEFOOT AREA

16. **5.8+** (5.?) ★ This goes up through the roof to the right of the thin crack, ending just right of a couple of small conifers.

17. **The Real Thing** (5.10a) ★★ A chimney/roof just across the road and swamp from *Sonny and Juanita*. There is a clump of birch just right of the top. The easiest way up this is probably only 5.9, but you won't find it the first time.

18. **Genetic Control** (5.13a) ★ Climb up into an alcove just left of *The Real Thing*, traverse onto the main face, and forge boldly up the middle of the curved upper section.

19. **Sizzlefoot** (5.12b) ★★★ About 20' left of *The Real Thing* you find a wooden culvert over the trail. This culvert points directly at *Sizzlefoot*, which often has wet ground at the base. Tie your shoes really tight for this 20-foot route.

20. **Little Sizzler** (5.10/5.12) ★/★★ Don't grease off! Climb the arete left of *Sizzlefoot* and exit left (5.10) or right to *Sizzlefoot* (5.12).

From the white pine near the top of The Real Thing look toward the river to see steps leading into another partial pothole. The next five routes are found therein.

21. **The Wheel** (5.9) Puzzle out a route to the left of *Lunge or Plunge* up to a little left-facing corner.

22. **Lunge or Plunge** (5.12-) ★ Climb the arching face left of *Schlocksides*. You can see a map of Minnesota in the rock—lunge for the Boundary Waters.

23. **Shlocksides** (5.9+) ★★ You can set up this and the next climb with one rope. This climb features a knee lock and several big jugs. Angle up right on jams from the left side of the pit.

24. **Slicksides** (5.9+) ★★★ Take the chalked-up crack on the right. The origin of the name is a profound mystery. A "direct" start is 5.11ish.

25. **Digitalis** (5.12-) To the right of the previous climb is an arete. This route passes right of the arete and left of a small, left-facing corner. Carefully pull the tree back with a sling and fire away. There are a couple of short boulder problems just to the right.

ANGLE ROCK

From the parking lot, the quickest approach is to stay on the asphalt and hang a left just before The Pit. Cross a bridge over The Boneyards (good bouldering) and climb up over the top to ledges leading down to the edge. I have tried to reunite the climbs with their original names as much as possible, but this little zone is particularly troublesome as far as names go.

26. **Barnacles and Backsides** (5.8+) There are some corners downstream of the ledge described on *Cosmos*. This route follows the largest of these corners.

27. **Thin Ice** (5.8+) A worthless short route. If you are still interested, drop down to the water at the eye bolt belay, climb a crack, then do the easy groove above. See, I told you.

**POTHOLES—
SLICKSIDES AREA**

ANGLE ROCK—EAST

ANGLE ROCK—NORTH

Sharon Williams on Cosmos.

28. **Cosmos** (5.10a) ★★ Work your way down right (Class 2) to the ledge with the eyebolt and belay there. Climb down the chimney, then climb the face just right of the easy groove. The crux is the funky basalt at the top.

29. **Witch's Tit, a.k.a. Requiem for a Swillhead** (5.10c) ★★★ The opportunity for variation is extensive on this climb. Here's one version: Start under a small overhang, right on a slight outside corner directly under the big overhang. Sequence your way up thin chips to a hold beneath the overhang, then skirt the overhang to the left. Harder variations could go directly over the roof.

30. **Iron Ring, a.k.a Witch's Tit** (5.10a) ★★ Climb just right of the iron ring to a ledge two-thirds of the way up. Now try to do the crux corner above.

31. **Stretcher** (5.11a-d) ★ Drop your rope from the triangular ledge left of the top of *Iron Ring*. Extend yourself desperately up the crack left of the *Vasectomy* arete. Difficulty is inversely proportional to the climber's height. Don't bother if you are less than 6' tall.

32. **Vasectomy** (5.11+) ★ Up the very crest of the arete right of *Stretcher*. The name comes from the consequences of blowing the first move, boys.

33. **Dirty Harry** (5.10b) Climb the face between *Vasectomy* and *Seat Broken*, using the arete occasionally.

34. **Seat Broken** (5.6) There are two left-facing corners on the north side of Angle Rock. This is the one closest to Wisconsin.

35. **Lichens and Spiders and Bears** (5.6) This wide crack is in the back of the left-facing corner closer to Minnesota.

PIECE OF CAKE AREA

MINNESOTA STRIP—RIGHT

LOOSE

40
VAR

38

40
VAR

The next two climbs are in the region of the upper boat dock.

36. **Slip Sliding Away, a.k.a. Candy's Impossible Crack** (5.9) ★ Just north of the upper boat landing.

37. **Political Wall** (5.9) ★ Just right of the previous climb.

MINNESOTA STRIP

This is probably the busiest bit of rock in the state. The top has traditionally been populated by tourists parking on U.S. Highway 8, but with the closure of the overlook the area is definitely more pleasant. From below, the top of the cliff can be reached by 1) taking the River Trail, which leads to the overlook from the service road (preferred); 2) hiking up and right from *Rosebush* to the overlook (eroded); or 3) scrambling up and left past #6 (watch for glass). Avoid the *Jammermeister* gully due to loose rock. As you walk up the talus from below, find an 8-foot block and maybe the stump of a basswood tree at the base of an obvious jam crack (*Piece of Cake*). Climbs are described from right to left.

38. **Station 62, a.k.a. Angel Food** (5.10c) ★★ Hopefully, some kid won't be dropping M&Ms on your head while you are climbing. This first decent climb on the main strip is a horizontal, two-foot roof with a finger/hand crack running through it. Scramble up to the base and climb it. You can cut left (5.9+) of the roof.

39. **Short Crack** (5.8) ★ Thirty feet right of Route 38 is a short finger crack above the eroded access gully.

Bruce McDonald on Fallen Knight.

40. **Rosebush** (5.5) ★★ A decent novice route, but it can be the site of falling rocks. About 15' right of the block at the base of *Piece of Cake* is a short face that leads to a dihedral capped by a small overhang. The corner just to the right offers good climbing as well, as does the difficult smooth face. The remainder of the cliff between here and *Station 62* is loose and trashy.

41. **Piece of Pie** (5.8) ★★★ Just right of Route 42 is an outside corner with a tiny roof. Follow this edge and try to avoid straying onto the following climb.

42. **Piece of Cake** (5.7-) ★★★ This well-worn crack doesn't live down to its name, especially for the novice leader. Start up the crack without using the big block. Follow the main crack as it widens, or weasel left onto easier terrain about halfway up. Leaders should sew up the bottom 20' (or your doctor may have to sew you up).

43. **Good Knight** (5.8) ★★ Up face to left of *Piece of Cake*. No, old-timer, this is not *Linden Tree Crack*.

44. **Armor All** (5.10) ★ Go up either side of the arete on typical Taylors Falls moves.

45. **Fallen Knight** (5.9) ★★★ The result of rockfall a few years ago. The day before, water was shooting out from the base of the slab as if there were an open fire hydrant. That night, climbers were climbing on *Black Knight* using headlamps. About 3 A.M. the slab cut loose, scaring the dickens out of the boat wranglers working on the paddlewheeler. Climb up the corner to easier ground, then finish as your setup permits. A harder finish exists on the arete near the top. FA: Nate Beckwith, et al.

46. **Sinister Midget** (5.?) Seven feet left of *Fallen Knight* is an overhanging bulge with a thin seam running through it. Surmount this to the horizontal overlap, then cut left or forge straight up. No known complete ascents.

47. **Death Gully** (5.0) Just Say No to this trash heap. I've seen several people hit by small stuff while standing at its base. Several major rockfalls have occurred here in the last 10 years (look up). 'Nuff said.

48. **Jammermeister** (5.5) ★★ If you actually do the last move, it's more like 5.6. At the top of the left-hand wall of the gully is a 15-foot crack. Get up to the base of this crack, preferably by using the flakes and ledges near the left edge of the wall, then climb the crack.

49. **Columeister** (5.6) ★★ Follow the dihedrals on the outside corner between *The Column* and *Jammermeister*.

50. **The Column** (5.6+) ★★★ The easiest tour of this climb is 5.6, but it is very easy to make it harder. Start in the dihedral to the left of the column. From the top of the column, go slightly left, watching for footholds and wasps as you go.

51. **The Column Direct** (5.9) ★★★ Put your foot on your ear and stand up. Straight up the face of the column, and don't use either edge, including that finger jam on the right. Continue above the column by staying to the right (5.8+, instead of the *voie normale* to the left).

52. **Blue Moon** (5.5) ★★★ Another good route for the neophyte. Just left of *The Column* is a roof about 20' up. Flit up under the right side of the roof, locate a couple of monstrous horizontal holds, move left, and go up the corner above. The roof offers a 5.7 exit to the right and a 5.9 when flashed directly.

53. **Nothing Fancy** (5.12b/c) ★ The first couple of holds are often chalked by climbers on the next route. Up the thin seam right of *Fancy Dancer*.

54. **Fancy Dancer** (5.11b) ★★★ More of a Gene Kelly climb, I think. Just right of #6 is a thin seam that leads to a block in the upper *Blue Moon* dihedral. Short people should look for the hold out to the left near the top, which is standard equipment on most of the hard climbs here.

55. **#6** (5.10a) ★★★ A Taylors Falls classic. Also known as *The Bulge*, it starts on the very left edge of the platform. Don't use the rocks to the left. Climb the thin crack up to and over the bulge. As you watch people fly up this, remember that they have already climbed it 156 times. FA (aid) and FFA: George Bloom.

56. **Urology** (5.8+) This route tries, and fails, to find good climbing on the wall left of #6.

57. **Devil's Chair** (5.9+) The Chair is now closed to climbing due to geological instability.

KEYHOLE AREA

From the old parking area above the Minnesota Strip, walk south along the highway for 200 feet to the next, smaller overlook. Peering over the front edge you see a ledge at the base of the artificial wall you are standing on. Reach this ledge by scrambling down from the north side of the overlook. This blocky ledge is the top of the Keyhole routes. Just south a few yards, a slightly detached buttress is the top of *Double Cracks* (best reached from below). *Reason to Believe* is on the main cliffline south of *Double Cracks*. Reach the bases of the routes by descending the loose chimney system just north of the overlook. From the base of the Keyhole face, note a wide slot (the Keyhole) just right of a rounded outside corner.

58. **The Horn** (5.7) Trend up and right to the right of *Keyhole*.

59. **Keyhole** (5.6) ★★ To unlock the easiest route of ascent, angle up and right past a pin to The Keyhole, then step right. Finish up the crack itself, often in the company of wasps.

60. **Keyhole Direct** (5.9) ★★★ Stay just left of the *Keyhole* crack, left of the arete, and avoid using any holds in the crack.

61. **Cobra, a.k.a. Keyhole Direct Direct** (5.11a) ★★★ Sternly limit yourself to the left side of this face for maximum difficulty.

62. **Double Cracks** (5.9–10) ★★ Though many folks (including myself) know this as *Hamburger Crack*, it was originally published as *Double Cracks*. On a slightly detached buttress just south of *Cobra* are two cracks facing the river. Using just one crack makes things a bit harder.

63. **Hamburger Helper** (5.7) ★ Look around to the left of the previous route. Climb the face, occasionally using the arete.

64. **Hamburger Crack** (5.9) A short crack in the corner.

65. **Reason to Believe** (5.11a) ★★ Some interesting moves make this a worthwhile objective. About 30' south of *Double Cracks* is a large cedar tree growing out of a chimney. Climb up right of the tree, traverse right onto a slab, and contemplate your next move. FA: Coleman Miller.

SECOND OVERLOOK AREA

This area has a few short climbs that are worth doing, especially on a hot, crowded weekend. Hike past the Keyhole Area to the wooden overlook that lies across from the Picnic Area rocks on the eastern side. Anchor to the rocks, not the overlook itself. Descend to the base to the north.

66. **Kornered** (5.8) ★ The arete right of the corner.

67. **Minihedral** (5.7) ★ A nice corner.

68. **Flopsy** (5.10a) ★ This is a mantle move over the lower roof.

KEYHOLE AREA—RIGHT

KEYHOLE
AREA—LEFT

SECOND OVERLOOK
AREA

69. **Digit Dance** (5.7) Start in an easy crack left of the roof. Traverse the slab left, then up the final crack above (loose). Variation: Mantle or face climb up to the left of the easy start (5.10-).

DELICATE DIHEDRAL AREA

These are the last worthwhile climbs on the Minnesota shore. The routes start a few yards downstream from the second overlook. Approaches are described for each climb.

70. **Charlie Tuna** (5.9) ★ Just before reaching the *Delicate Dihedral* descent gully is a face with a couple of small overhangs. Walk around and you can get a view of it from the various overlooks, or from the top of *Dogleg Crack*.

71. **Dogleg Crack** (5.4) ★★ The only problem is that it is too short. Finding it is the hard part. From the base of *Delicate Dihedral*, work upstream across the descent gully. A face leads to a crack cutting through an overhang. When finished, you will be right (north) of *Charlie Tuna*.

Delicate Dihedral and its variations are found at the bottom of a ridge that starts about 150 feet south of the Second Overlook. Options for reaching these climbs include descending the gully just north of the ridge (5th class) or descending ledges above *Dogleg Crack* (4th class Tarzan swings on trees).

DELICATE DIHEDRAL AREA—CHARLIE TUNA

DELICATE BUTTRESS

The routes left of the main dihedral were formerly known collectively as the *Obscure Cracks*; I could find no names for the individual routes. The ridge itself can be done as a couple of pitches.

72. **Delicate Dihedral** (5.8) ★★ The easiest version takes a crack on the right side of the face up to a ledge. Step across to footholds above the overhang. Variations: Lieback the corner, exit left (5.7) or straight up (5.11ish).

73. **Feather Jam** (5.7-) ★ Right of the fin, left of the lieback corner. Start up the slab, use the thin crack to reach the upper cracks.

74. **Fowl Pro** (5.8+) ★★ Go directly up the offwidth without using the fin or the thin crack.

75. **Wake Me Up** (5.6) ★ To the left of the fin, yawn up cracks through a couple of lieback moves near the top.

76. **Cutting Edge** (5.9) Good luck finding this. On the south wall of the *Delicate Dihedral* ridge, near the top.

77. **Thumbs Up** (5.7) ★ Just south of the *Delicate Dihedral* ridge is a gully and a prow of rock. *Thumbs Up* climbs up the face below. You can make it harder, I suppose.

WISCONSIN

Wisconsin offers climbers a more diverse selection of routes than the Minnesota side. The Wisconsin unit is much larger and includes approaches that are (gasp) up to ten minutes long. The combination of north-facing rock, moss, and trees can provide a cool respite even on the hottest summer days.

All of the Wisconsin routes are most easily approached by driving into the park. From the U.S. Highway 8 bridge over the St. Croix River, proceed into Wisconsin and drive up the hill. Go south on Wisconsin Highway 35 for 0.3 mile and turn into the park on the right. A valid Minnesota Parks pass is honored on weekdays; weekends you must pay the going rate. Federal Golden Eagle cards are honored at all times and are available at the St. Croix Wild and Scenic River office in St. Croix Falls, Wisconsin.

It is also possible to walk over from the Minnesota side, although this is only sensible if you are going to the Wisconsin Strip area. A telephone and water are available at the building just uphill from the Wisconsin Strip parking area. Bathrooms are located at the interpretive center, beach, and the picnic grounds.

WISCONSIN STRIP

This area holds the largest concentration of good routes on this side. Consequently, it is very busy. Large numbers of tourists hike the Pothole Trail and peer over the edge while you're cursing at the crux. Approach these climbs by parking at the Pothole Trail parking area (the first intersection past the interpretive center). Take the left fork of the trail and hike until you have passed a

WISCONSIN STRIP OVERVIEW

wooden overlook. This should put you at the top of some cliffs with a two-foot diameter pothole nearby. You are now above *Outside Corner* and *Rurp City*. To reach Route 78, turn right and hike toward the bridge.

To reach the bottoms of the rest of the climbs, proceed north past the pothole for a few feet to a blocky gully. Descend the gully to a block with a tree (be nice to this old friend), then downclimb (Class 3) an 8-foot wall and slither down the slab. Some folks are dropping a sling down this wall. Don't do this unless you intend to tie in; it's too hard to hold onto if you slip.

At times of high water, it may be difficult to cross the area beneath *Inside Corner*. Park rangers patrol this area often, so it is to your advantage not to have slings crossing the main trail, or to have your food and drink prominently displayed.

78. **Octagenarian** (5.10+) Across from the upper boat dock, directly out of the water. A couple of big blocks lie on top of the small buttress.

79. **Softer than Ice, Harder than Diamonds** (5.13+) ★ This route works up the very left edge of the *Deuchler's Corner* face. FA: Chris Ecklund.

80. **Deuchler's Corner Left** (5.12b-d) ★★★ The exact line of the original route is probably not that important. There are several interchangeable parts (see photo); do what you like. Going straight up the thin crack on the north face is reachy and may provide a B2 move for you.

81. **Deuchler's Corner Center** (5.11b/c) ★★★ Shorter folks may need a dynamic personality to get started up this version. Start near the top of the approach slab and ape up right to the first hold, then go up (not right), finishing on the left side of the arete.

WISCONSIN STRIP—LEFT

82. **Deuchler's Corner Right** (5.10c) ★★★ Start the same as the previous version, but chicken out right to the stance. Now haul up left of the corner to the crack, move right and pull the roof just right of the arete.

83. **Walking on Air, a.k.a. The Honeywell Project** (5.10b) ★★★ The bottom moves used to be hard before sticky rubber. From the base of the large block, traverse straight left, then up on thin holds to a stance on the left side of the face. Pull up a short crack and move a bit left to finish just right of the arete. A direct start (5.10b-d) can be found directly below the ledge, using holds on the corner to swing up and right to the bracket. A direct finish is 5.11b. FA: Dick Wildberger and Dan Kieffaber, 1975.

84. **Batman** (5.10b) ★★★ Make sure your utility belt is buckled correctly. From the top of the column, move left through the overhang and head for a small roof at the top of the face, using a couple of wiggly holds. Originally this was known as *Facelift*, and *Batman* referred to the face left of *Lloyd's Lament*.

85. **Lloyd's Lament** (5.6) ★ As climbers destroy the soil at the top, this climb is getting cleaner, and the tree has died. Stem up the left-facing corner/chimney (I assume Lloyd was lamenting about the last couple of moves), or follow the face just to the left.

86. **Rurp City** (5.12b/c) ★★ Starting from a small talus block, levitate up the center of this north-facing wall to the top of the red streaks, diagonal left, and power up to the second crux. You can avoid the opening moves by starting in the corner to the left, but I wouldn't admit to it.

87. **Outside Corner** (5.5) ★★ The next three routes share a common start at the base of the dihedral. *Outside Corner* outwits the upper roof to the left. A good route for the novice, but watch for pendulums on the top-rope setup.

88. **Split the Difference** (5.9–5.10b) ★ Contrived but fun. Go through the middle of the roof, avoiding the good holds to the left. The truly honed will lay off some small chips to the right to earn the 10b merit badge.

89. **Inside Corner** (5.8) ★★★ Many aspiring leaders find themselves in an unfortunate jam at the roof. As you throw your hand into the bomber crack above, remember that bats occasionally roost there.

90. **The Old Man** (5.8-) ★★★ The next two climbs are reminiscent of Eldorado Canyon and offer nice face climbing. The upper left edge of this wall looks like an old man in profile. Follow the face holds just right of the sharp arete.

91. **Cathuseleft** (5.10b) ★★ Try to stay in the seam to the right of *The Old Man*.

92. **Cathuselum** (5.7) ★★★ The crux is the last 5' (a jamcrack), but many novices have trouble on the face moves below . Start just left of the jamcrack and weave up the lower-angle, dark face. This route can be done with one hand.

93. **Mother** (5.4) ★ The easiest route in this area but seldom done due to its brevity.

94. **Dire Straits** (5.9) ★ Thrash up through the vegetation just right of *Mother* and follow a flake to the crux—the transition from overhanging to underhanging.

95. **Impossible Crack** (5.9+) ★★ Hint: Always try this when you are out of shape, injured, hung over, etc. About 20' right of the large block at the base of *Cathuselum* you will find a short, hanging offwidth crack. Try to stay in it. There is a 5.12 face to the left.

96. **Chimney Left** (5.4) The crack on the left face of the chimney.

97. **Chimney** (5.4) The chimney itself.

98. **Triple Overhang** (5.11a) ★★★ South of *Impossible Crack* are a gully and a slabby face. Flow up the face without using either edge. Height-dependent, with steep face moves. First (and hopefully last) lead: T. Deuchler.

99. **Slab Route** (5.6) ★ A corner and slab system right of the previous route goes up, right, and up.

100. **Joint Project** (5.13a) ★★★ From the base of *Triple Overhang*, look up and right to an attractive, north-facing face. There are several variations.

ROD'S AREA

These routes are located below the stone parapet along the road between the Wisconsin Strip and the Sentinel Area. Park as for the Wisconsin Strip, hike south along the road to a set of steps leading down through the retaining wall. A cedar stump lies about five feet right of the top of *Skin of Rod's Teeth*.

ROD'S AREA

101. **Crossover Artist** (5.11) ★ Start near the junction of the wall with the river. Start with a slightly overhanging face, then up a finger crack to a very interesting exit over a bulge. Finish up an easier hand crack.

102. **Skin of Rod's Teeth** (5.10) ★★★ An excellent finger crack that starts from a platform just above the water.

103. **Edge Lane** (5.10+) ★★★ The arete right of *Rod's*.

104. **Thrombus** (5.8) ★ This flared crack is a good place for gym climbers to learn the meaning of the phrase "trad 5.8." It's also similar to the crux pitches on most of the routes in the Steck and Roper book, *50 Classic Climbs of North America*.

105. **Mickey Mantles** (5.9) ★ Right of *Thrombus*, up several ledges.

106. **Mental Physics** (5.10) ★★ A black, licheny strip leads to a small roof, then up near a seam.

107. **Hand Jive** (5.12) ★ Four feet right of *Mental Physics*, climb past a horizontal hand jam.

Note: There are some short routes that lie between the road and the Sentinel Area.

SENTINEL AREA

These climbs face roughly north and are across from the lower boat dock on the Minnesota side. Park at the Summit Rock Trail parking area, just before you reach the beach. The best approach takes the major trail that proceeds slightly north into the woods.

Take the right fork (Summit Rock Trail), pass along a short cliff on the left, and reach some wooden steps to your left. Ascend the steps, hike past some oaks, and reach the tops of the climbs just before another set of wooden steps (going down). The top of *Sentinel* is marked by a double crack that faces the Minnesota Potholes, while *Yosemite Crack* ends on a ledge below and to the right.

To reach the bases of *Sentinel* and *Yosemite Crack*, continue down the steps to the south end of the railings. Cut north on the rocks back toward *Sentinel*. When the top part of *Sentinel* comes into view, go down left a few feet (near a white pine) and downclimb into a short corner. Continue down and around a few more feet to a nice but exposed ledge with a large tree. This is the top of *Lost Ego* and the belay point for *Sentinel* and *Yosemite Crack*. This approach is Class 3 and can be very slippery. With a big tree close by, consider a quick belay for those with less experience.

108. **Lost Ego** (5.8-) ★★★ From the base of *Sentinel*, pick your way down the gully to the north. Then climb the crack/face right back up to where you started. A decent lead if you have a large camming unit.

109. **Lost Eagle** (5.8) Climb the crack system around the corner right of *Lost Ego*.

110. **Stay Hungry** (5.10b) ★ Just left of *Yosemite Crack*. A route called *AIDS* (5.11) is somewhere farther left under the shrubbery and lichens.

111. **Yosemite Crack** (5.10a) ★★★ Seems obvious until you stick your hand in the crack. To create a truly schizophrenic climb, first squirm up the face below (5.10a).

112. **Unknown** (5.?) The face that rises above the *Yosemite* setup ledge has a line of unknown difficulty.

113. **Sentinel Crack** (5.10a) ★★★ One of the best routes in the area. Swing past a dead treelet to double cracks and dream of a full pitch like the top 20 feet.

The next five routes are found above and south of the Sentinel Area. The bases of the routes are reached by climbing down a short chimney at the south end of the wooden railing.

114. **Unknown** (5.?) ★ The arete left of *Captain Coconuts*.

115. **Captain Coconuts** (5.10b) ★★★ This climb is found above and south of the Sentinel Area. After leaving the trail to approach *Sentinel Crack*, note a clean prow of rock that extends toward the river. This prow forms the south-facing wall of a large corner. The route goes up this face, about 4' left of the corner.

116. **Cordless Electric Pus Melon** (5.9+) The face below *Captain Coconuts*.

117. **Das Boot** (5.10b/c) ★★ Just around to the right from the base of *Captain Coconuts* is a short rock with an overhang low and a sharp arete above. This route climbs up the left side of the overhang and prow to a hold on the junction between two faces.

118. **The Prow** (5.12a) ★★★ Start under the right (west) side and proceed up under the triangular face. Use holds on the right side of the triangle, grab the prow, and continue.

INDIAN HEAD

This area can be approached in a couple of different ways. The closest approach is to hike past the beach along the north shore of Lake o' the Dalles. Take the first right-hand fork, which is the Echo Canyon Trail. Go past a small pond, pass some cliffs on your left, and reach stone steps that descend to the river. Indian Head is the cliff on your left. A human profile can be seen from certain directions.

119. **Little Wing** (5.4) ★★ On the south (uphill) side of the buttress is a right-facing corner. Climb the face to the right, with the crux just off the ground.

120. **Indian Head** (5.8) ★ Just right of the prow is a right-facing corner with a jagged crack to the right. Take the easiest finish up and left.

121. **Air Conditioned** (5.7) ★★ Everybody wants to be the belayer on a hot July day. Up the cool crack, trending left, past somewhat loose blocks to the top.

Sean McCoy leading Sentinel Crack, *a Taylors Falls classic.* PHOTO BY STEPHEN REGENOLD

SENTINEL AREA

THE PROW

118

INDIAN HEAD

122. **Layback, a.k.a. Heatwave** (5.8) ★★★ Just left of Route 121, take the deceptive lieback crack and continue up the small dihedral above.

123. **Mantrap** (5.10c/d) ★★ Folks of either sex are likely to have trouble on the first crux, and the overhanging wall above isn't much easier. A roof is found about 15' up, right of Route 121. Try to get up into the corner, try to surmount the roof (don't cheat right), then try the wall above, again without cheating, onto easier ground.

124. **Wise Crack** (5.8) ★ Thirty to 80 feet right of *Mantrap* are several corners and cracks of various difficulty, all short. This is the best-looking one and has a tree and a roof.

BOAT PEOPLE ROCK

About 100 feet downriver from the previous climbs is a tall crag with a mossy slab at its base (very evident from the Minnesota side as you approach the lower boat landing). A prominent prow juts out to the left of the slab. Again, names are a problem here.

125. **Boat People** (5.9+) Takes the black face to the left of the prow (from below). See *Atlas Shrugged*.

126. **Frequent Flyer** (5.11) ★ The arete.

127. **Atlas Shrugged** (5.10+) ★★ Take the slightly overhanging face above a higher ledge to the right of the prow. This was incorrectly called *Boat People* in my previous guide.

128. **Holiday in Cambodia** (5.10+) Up the face to a tree and ledge, then climb *Atlas Shrugged*.

BOAT PEOPLE ROCK

126

127

LEDGE

128

IMPORTANT: CLOSED AREAS

The area immediately south of the previous routes is closed to visitors. This includes *Unseemly* and the routes around *The Cross*. Climbers are obeying the closure; cliff jumpers are not.

PICNIC AREA

These short routes might offer some unoccupied rock on a crowded day. They lie just south of the closed area. To reach them, drive back to the picnic grounds by the river and park as close to the boat launch as possible. Hike up and right toward the Riverbluff Trail. Stay on the official trail, eventually reaching the edge of the cliffs. The easiest approach to the base leaves the trail at this point, goes downhill 15' to a three-stemmed birch and proceeds upriver.

To reach the tops of the climbs, go instead up the steps to the right and proceed until you see two prows of rock jutting out. The first prow is the top of *Electric Stove Couch* and the second prow is the top of *Pine Tree*. Across the river is a wooden overlook with a short cliff below it. Past these prows are signs marking the closed area. It is possible to descend (Class 3) just north of the tops of the climbs.

129. **Rock Dove, a.k.a. Picnic Crack Left** (5.6) ★ The left edge of the face is bounded by this somewhat irritating crack.

130. **Pine Tree, a.k.a. Picnic Face** (5.10a) ★★ This route is no free lunch. March straight up the delicate face.

131. **Picnic Crack Right** (5.8+) ★★ Leadable, but a bit sporting. Start up the cracks, traverse left, then up over the little roof.

132. **Picnic Edge** (5.8) From the top of the cracks on the previous route, work up the arete above.

133. **Trash Patrol** (5.6) The wide crack right of *Picnic Edge*. Watch for broken glass.

134. **Electric Stove Couch** (5.7–5.10d) ★ Around to the right of Picnic Face is a right-facing dihedral with a big roof at the top. Do the corner and sneak left for the 5.7 version. Or, horse up over the roof for the harder version.

135. **Grishnakh or Gorbag** (5.7) A right-facing corner 90' right of the previous route.

Bob Myers on Dance of the Sugar-Plump Faeries, *Shovel Point.*

NO CHALK AREA

THE NORTH SHORE

Northern Minnesota was first explored by Europeans over 300 years ago. One of the most noted of these explorers was Daniel Graysolon, Sieur du Lhut, who left Montreal in 1678 for the great Northwest (today's Minnesota, Wisconsin, and Ontario). During the next two decades Du Lhut managed to make peace with the northern tribes, rescue Father Louis Hennepin from a band of Sioux, and build Fort Kaministiquia in Ontario. His most outlandish act may have been (with the help of a handful of other Europeans) the pursuit of two natives accused of murder into their tribe's camp, followed by a trial and execution, all while surrounded by the presumably irate defendants' relatives.

When the fur trade died off in the mid 1800s, it was briefly replaced by a rush to mine copper and even gold. While this didn't pan out, both iron ore and timber did prove to be economic booms for the region. At one time, the great freighters moved 50 million tons of iron ore a year across the lake. In 1902, a new company was formed to mine anorthosite near Ilgen City (just east of Tettegouche State Park) for use as an abrasive. The venture failed, and the company's stock soon was traded at "two shares for a shot, and cheap whiskey at that." However, Minnesota Mining and Manufacturing (3M) seems to have recovered nicely from this early setback. Today, the great white pine forests are gone and taconite mining waxes and wanes, so tourism currently provides many Arrowhead residents with their livelihood.

The area of Minnesota from Duluth eastward is known as the Arrowhead region. Duluth has about anything you might need, including scheduled air and bus service. Currently, two stores stock climbing gear in Duluth: Ski Hut and Continental Ski and Sports.

Minnesota Highway 61 (MN 61) runs along the North Shore from Duluth to the Canadian border. It serves as a major truck route and is usually jammed with campers and other tourists. During the fall color season (late September–early October) traffic can be especially nasty. The character of the road is changing; the state is widening and straightening more and more of the road, and tunnels replace the dangerous curves on Silver Cliff. This results in more and more traffic (which will lead to more roadwork, etc.).

Most of the locals are very friendly. There are, however, more than a few folks who seem to be prepared to shoot down the black UN helicopters that are coming to establish a new world order, if you catch my drift. The NO TRES-PASSING signs usually mean just that, and I'd advise an apologetic retreat if you are told to clear out, even if you think you are on public land. This won't be a problem if you stick to the areas listed in this guide. Seekers of new crags are advised to contact landowners prior to any exploration.

Another type of unfriendly development has arisen (and will become more common, I'm sure). This is the "elite retreat" development, which buys up land, then closes the cliffs to climbing. The Baptism Wall is now part of the White Tail Ridge Subdivision, and climbing (or even trail access) is not permitted. Do not drive or park on their road.

The fall is the nicest time to climb on the North Shore; the leaves are changing, the humidity is down, the bugs have decreased—but the hunters are out! Any area outside of the State Parks should be considered a hunting zone after Labor Day. A blaze orange vest weighs nothing and provides some peace of mind in these situations. Plan something else on the first day of deer season in any given area. The Superior Hiking Trail Association recommends staying out of the woods during firearms deer season (check the dates each year).

Some general comments about climbing on the North Shore. Three of the main areas (Palisade Head, Shovel Point, and Carlton Peak) are covered under the Minnesota Climbing Management Plan (MNCMP). Read the information carefully in each section, and register yearly at the appropriate park offices. The crags in the Mystical Mountain Zone are owned primarily by the Wolf Ridge Environmental Learning Center. Wolf Ridge is sympathetic to climbing, but there are some access rules—again, be familiar with these.

Evacuations and emergency care are coordinated by the sheriff of each county. Keep in mind that high-angle rock rescues are not common, so rescue teams may not be much more knowledgeable than the climbers at hand. I hope that you feel a responsibility to help in any rescue to the best of your ability, and I hope that you will help if you are qualified to do so. For the inexperienced, many hands are needed for nontechnical tasks, such as carrying equipment and stretchers.

Pay attention to the rock type at the areas you visit, as they differ in climbing and protection characteristics. Hexes and cams are both useful, and leaders should be arrayed with an adequate assortment of gear for wide cracks. Use caution when tying off trees growing in the thin soil of the cliff edges and remember that small birches are manky anchors (see page 3 for more on trees). Anorthosite can eat ropes and slings; bring padding or rope tubes to safeguard your investment and your life. A fixed rap line is useful at several areas.

North Shore ethics have traditionally allowed significant gardening, but not placement of fixed pins or bolts. Unfortunately, the impressive aid climbs on Palisade Head are probably not feasible due to the state's prohibition against nailing. Clean aid aficionados, please prove me wrong.

Route names and grades of old aid climbs were based on those in *Superior Climbs*, by Dave Pagel, illustrated by Rick Kollath. This guidebook has been out of print for many years; a new version will hopefully be out by the time you read this. Dave's eloquence and Rick's amazing drawings have set a standard that is hard to meet. If you see their guide, buy it.

NO CHALK AREA

NORTH SHORE OVERVIEW

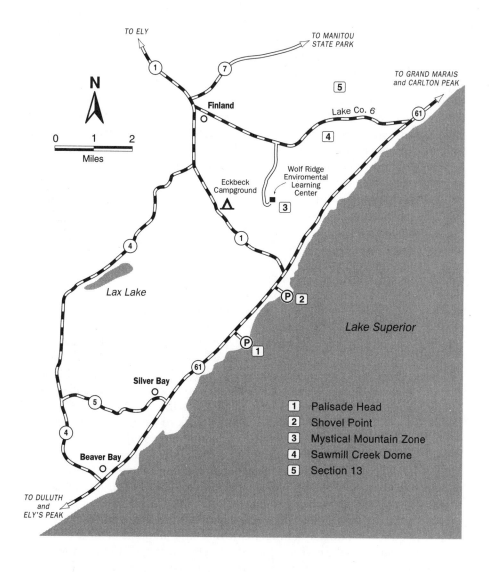

TO ELY

TO MANITOU
STATE PARK

TO GRAND MARAIS
and CARLTON PEAK

5

Finland

Lake Co. 6

61

4

N

0   1   2
Miles

Eckbeck
Campground

Wolf Ridge
Enviromental
Learning
Center

3

1

4

Lax Lake

P 2

Lake Superior

P 1

61

Silver Bay

5

4

Beaver Bay

1 Palisade Head
2 Shovel Point
3 Mystical Mountain Zone
4 Sawmill Creek Dome
5 Section 13

TO DULUTH
and
ELY'S PEAK

CHALK

The Short Version: The North Shore has had a no-chalk ethic for nearly 30 years. Respect this local tradition and do not use chalk on North Shore crags.

The Long Version: Just north of Duluth, the Laurentian Divide forms a major watershed boundary that separates water flowing north to the Arctic Ocean from water flowing into the Atlantic Ocean. Duluth itself straddles the Magnesium Carbonate Divide, a watershed of sorts that separates two areas having distinct climbing ethics. South of Duluth, the use of chalk is an accepted part of climbing; the North Shore ethic is different.

North Shore climbers adopted a "no chalk" ethic in the 1970s. Dave Pagel devoted over 2,000 words to this topic in the second edition of *Superior Climbs*, laying out the rationale against chalk usage in a fatherly but firm way. Since most of you don't have that guide, here's a summary. Chalk usage is a visual eyesore to almost everyone (climbers included), and this threatens climbing access to the cliffs. The no-chalk ethic that developed here is part of a larger ethic of environmental respect, and voluntary control of chalk use is far better than government regulation.

Let me add a couple of reasons for not using chalk. I remember the first time I did *Ross's Crack* on Shovel Point. As I hit the crux, I looked around for holds—but then I realized that I was actually looking for chalk, not at the rock itself. I was forced to puzzle out the moves in the same way the first ascentionists did rather than follow the white smears. Those of you who learned to climb indoors may find it strange to be concerned about this, since routefinding consists of looking for colored tape instead of solving the puzzles posed by nature. Believe me, that's not the way it's supposed to be and your experience is diminished as a result.

Using chalk also puts those cooperating with local ethics at a disadvantage. One Twin Cities climber waited nearly two years to try an onsight flash of *Sacred Biscuit*. He swung through the crux, grabbed a heavily chalked hold, and slipped off. He was prevented from reaching his goal by the selfish acts of others. Climb at Devil's Lake or Taylors Falls some day without chalk to see what I mean.

While the North Shore has a no-chalk ethic, most of the climbers in the United States have decided that chalk is ethically OK. Indeed, many southern Minnesota and Wisconsin climbers feel that North Shore climbers have no right to dictate how people climb on public lands, and that chalk is far less damaging than bolting or nailing (which permanently alters the rock).

As a biologist, I find the concept of aggressive cleaning to be far more heinous than either chalking or bolting. Removing large amounts of loose material and vegetation alters the cliff ecosystem in a permanent way; to my knowledge there is no scientific evidence to show that chalk damages the rock. Given the need for gardening along the North Shore (admittedly necessary if climbing is to be done on some cliffs), the anti-chalk ethic can only be defended on aesthetic and political grounds, not on an environmental basis.

Some of you will follow this ethic without further discussion. Some of you will disregard it regardless of the arguments (I'll deal with those folks below).

NO CHALK AREA

The rest of you may be trying to make up your mind on the issue. When you struggle to resolve an ethical dilemma in climbing, I suggest that certain arguments are more powerful than others, in this order:

(1) Environmental ethics (strongest)

(2) Laws and rules

(3) Local ethics

(4) National ethics

(5) Personal choice (weakest)

Environmental concerns overrule any other argument, while personal choice is the weakest stance to take. In other words, when there is a conflict between local and national ethics, local ethics should be followed. While local ethics have allowed piton placement at Palisade, state rules prohibit that now—so we climb hammerless. In the case of chalk, local ethics say no chalk. An ethical climber won't use chalk while climbing along the North Shore, even though it doesn't follow his or her personal choice. Sometimes the benefits to many outweigh the costs to a few.

Here's the big problem. We live in an era where personal freedom and individuality seem to reign supreme. The "Me-First" attitude has little room for respect, tradition, or other points of view. Personal choice becomes paramount—"I wanna use chalk" overrides local ethics, State Park recommendations, and accepted environmental ethics in the area. Who cares about anybody else, or future access to the cliffs? All that matters is what I want, and I want it now! Nobody has a right to tell me what to do, it's a free country. . . . Sorry, I thought I was on talk radio. Anyway, this attitude is quite widespread (and quite shortsighted).

There is a very simple solution for the Me-First crowd. If you don't agree with the no-chalk ethic, climb elsewhere. Devil's Lake, Blue Mounds, Taylors Falls, Red Wing, and your local rock gym are all options if chalk is more important to you than other climbers or continued access to the crags in the future.

> On that occasion [Willo Welzenbach] and Karl Wein, arriving in Austria on a Saturday morning after a tiresome overnight rail journey from Munich, cycled some 20 kilometers up the Fusch Valley and crossed a pass involving 1,600 metres of ascent to reach the hut serving as a base for their route. With a 2:30 A.M. start on Sunday, they completed their intricate 1,400 metres of ascent [the first, of the Grossglockner North Face], in which the face of 600 metres is now recognized as one of the hardest mixed climbs in the Eastern Alps, and returned to base by dusk. Assisted by a full moon, they re-crossed the pass to the Fusch Valley that evening and cycled down to the railway station to catch the night train back to Munich.
> —Eric Roberts, *Welzenbach's Climbs*

ELYS PEAK OVERVIEW

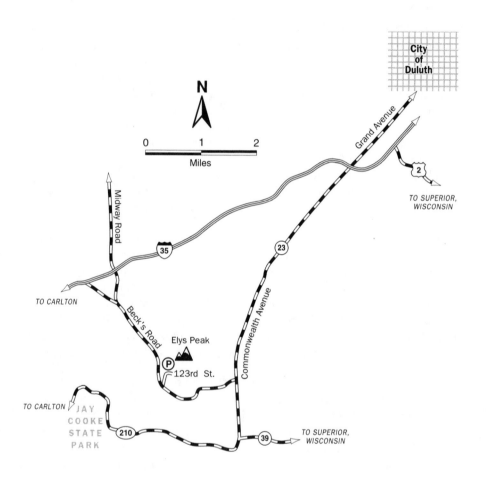

NO CHALK AREA

ELYS PEAK

The first-time visitor to Elys Peak will start salivating in the parking lot. The crag seems large and there seems to be ample opportunity for new routes. A ten-minute walk to the base of Tunnel Bluff shatters both illusions–the climbs are fairly short and the unclimbed rock is not worth the bother. Nevertheless, it's a good place for locals to catch a pump and for visitors from the south to start their North Shore trips if they get there in the late afternoon. It also seems quite popular with the Kiddy Kamps who take their young charges climbing.

Emergency contact: Dial 911 or contact the St. Louis County Sheriff. The nearest pay phone is in New Duluth. Take Beck's Road (St. Louis County Road 3) to Minnesota Highway 23, then go right for 2 miles to the Amoco station. Hospitals are available in Duluth (Exit at Mesaba Avenue off Interstate 35 and follow signs).

The climbing environment: Elys Peak is owned by the City of Duluth and has no specific climbing regulations. A couple of bolt routes appeared and disappeared on the Northwestern Bluff. Recall the "no bolt" ethic on the North Shore. Let's not have any bolt wars, please. The rock is basalt, and Taylors Falls expatriates will find themselves right at home. There is a no-chalk ethic in the area; please respect it.

Services: Jay Cooke State Park (busy in the summer) offers camping, and private campgrounds are also available. The closest services are in New Duluth, 1.7 miles east to MN 23 and then south. Duluth is less than 10 miles away. Other local attractions include the Munger Trail for biking and inline skating, Jay Cooke State Park, The Duluth Zoo (off MN 23, south of Interstate 35). See Appendix A for more information.

Approach: Elys Peak lies between Duluth and Carlton, not far off Interstate 35. From I–35, go south on Midway Road (Exit 246). Midway Road merges into Beck's Road after 0.6 mile. Continue south past the quarry until you cross a bridge at 2.2 miles. Turn left on 123rd St. (2.6 miles) and drive to the obvious parking area before reaching the Munger Bike Trail.

From Duluth, exit I–35 on MN 23 (exit 251B). Drive south past the zoo, the Superior National Forest Headquarters, and reach a railroad bridge 4.8 miles south of I–35. Just south of the railroad bridge, turn west onto Beck's Road. Drive 1.7 miles to 123rd Street, turn right, and continue to the parking lot.

From the parking lot the rocks are evident. Turn right on the bike trail for about 50 yards and take the obvious wide trail to the left (not the narrow trail through the fence). Cross the field and the railroad tracks, then huff up the hill to the old railroad bed. If you don't see a railroad tunnel on your right, you're lost. From here, your route depends on your goal.

Across from the railroad bed three trails may be seen. The leftmost trail is level at the start and leads to a spur trail to the Northwestern Bluff. The middle trail starts about 20 feet right of the level trail and climbs uphill to the main area, the West Face of Tunnel Bluff. The right hand trail climbs steeply and leads somewhere, I suppose. A fourth option is to go through the tunnel to reach the East Face of Tunnel Bluff. A few obscure routes can be found there (but are not listed here).

TUNNEL BLUFF, WEST FACE

The highest concentration of easy climbs and shortest approach make this the popular spot. A nasty gully to the left of *Cakewalk* is the standard approach to the top. This gully is loose and steep at the top, and I'd think twice about climbing below anyone. A more solid alternative lies a couple of minutes farther left, to the right of *Royal Robbins F12 Overhang*.

1. **Royal Robbins F12 Overhang** (5.8) ★★ A corner and overhang to the left of gully north (left) of the main access gully. FA: Dave and Jim Mital.

2. **Cakewalk** (5.5) ★ Just right of the main approach gully. FA: D. and J. Mital.

3. **Simple Corner** (5.3) ★ What more is there to say? A right-facing corner with few challenges. FA: D. and J. Mital.

4. **Static is a Four-Letter Word** (5.10b) ★ Reach for the sky, pardner. Stay between the previous and next route. FA: D. and J. Mital.

5. **Beginner's Crack** (5.6) ★ Short and sorta sweet. Jam up 'til you can jam no more. FA: D. and J. Mital.

TUNNEL BLUFF—WEST FACE

NO CHALK AREA

6. **New Corner** (5.5) ★ The prominent left-facing corner. FA: D. and J. Mital.

7. **Bionic Finger Crack** (5.12a) ★★★ A classic, if such a short climb can be considered one. Vault up to the base of the crack and sketch upward. FA: Dave Pagel.

8. **Dislocation Overhang** (5.6) ★★★ Act like you're heading for the 5.12, then cut right up the lieback. FA: Steve Mabley.

9. **Jigsaw** (5.8) ★ Up the face just right of the previous climb.

NORTHWESTERN BLUFF

A handful of decent, moderately hard routes with reasonable access. Take the level, left-hand trail from the abandoned railroad grade, passing a rock with an eye bolt on your left. After about 90 paces, the trail meets the edge of a small streambed, where a faint trail cuts across the stream. Follow this trail for a couple of minutes to the right end of the wall. Walk left past a protruding buttress to the left side of a brushy area. An obvious gully goes up and right to the top. The far right end of the rock can be reached via bushwacking, if you wish. Routes are described from right to left, as you encounter them on the approach.

10. **Two Right Feet** (5.9) ★ At the right end of the wall to the right of *The Flake*. FA: Rick Kollath.

11. **Coming Unhinged** (5.10d) ★★ Climb right of a small roof just right of *The Flake*, then proceed upward to a small left-facing corner. FA: Dave Pagel.

Bruce McDonald on Corner Geometry.

12. **The Flake** (5.7) ★★★ Feets don't fail me now. A jagged crack works up and right, eventually meeting the main corner. FA: Steve Mabley.

13. **The Bulge** (5.8) ★★★ A corner/crack system passes a ledge to a distinct right-facing corner halfway up. FA: Steve Mabley.

14. **The Boys of Summer** (5.10c) ★★ This route and the next two are found on a buttress just left of *The Flake*. Just left of *The Bulge* is a roof. Over the left side of this, aim for the small dihedral above. FA: Brian Gitar.

15. **Take Two, They're Small** (5.10b) ★ Start under a block that forms a small roof; there's a thin crack running up the left side of the block. From the top of the block go more or less straight up. FA: Dave Pagel and Steve Mankenberg.

16. **Kindly Step Aside** (5.10a) ★★ Work up the left side of the buttress, using an undercling near the bottom. FA: Dave Pagel.

17. **Corner Geometry** (5.6) ★★ A large right-facing corner on the left side of the access gully. Not a bad lead.

18. **Open Your Wrist or Slit Your Throat** (5.11) To the left of *Corner Geometry* find a thin crack starting off the ground. Reach it, then climb it.

Mark Morrissey on Urge to Mate, *Palisade Head.*

NO CHALK AREA

PALISADE HEAD

The climbing at Palisade Head can have an air of seriousness not found anywhere else between the Rockies and New England. The fickle moods of the lake and winds define your experience, which may range from idyllic, bug-free sunshine to clammy fog to pounding waves and snow squalls. Somehow, the climbing experience often seems a bit more complete here than it does down south.

The lake makes its own weather. No matter what time of year you visit, be prepared for cold, wet conditions. Many ships have gone to a watery grave "when the gales of November come early," to quote Gordon Lightfoot. Luckily, no climbers have suffered a similar fate. Fogbanks can swoop in seemingly between moves, and squalls may pounce from any direction. Weather forecasts are useful only as a general guide, as conditions may change with each bend in the shoreline.

Emergency contact: Call 911 or contact the park office. The nearest phones are in Silver Bay (gas station at the stoplight) and at the Tettegouche Rest Area. For campers on Minnesota State Highway 1 (MN 1), there is one pay phone in Finland, on the south side of the grocery store. Report all accidents to the park office.

The climbing environment: The issue of chalk was discussed in the North Shore introduction (see p. 192). If you skipped over that section, go back and read it now. This area is part of Tettegouche State Park, so a valid permit is required if you intend to stay more than one hour. Also, please register each year at the park headquarters.

The base of Palisade Head is about the only place in the Midwest that a climber can be seriously marooned. Heavy surf and/or ice can make the talus impassable, cutting off your escape route. In doubtful weather, a strategically placed fixed line (and the skill to use it) can provide peace of mind. *Southern Escape Gully* (5.0), *Dirty Harry* (5.7), and *Northern Escape Chimney* (5.8 or 5.0) are the best upward retreats if one must climb out. A short fixed rope in the boulder cave at the south edge of the Amphitheater ain't a bad idea if you intend to pass through more than once.

Loose rock is a major concern, especially from the North Tower northward. We're talking big chunks here, not pebbles. Some of these climbs see very little action and you can expect to find killer blocks and flakes delicately poised and waiting for the unwary. There have been at least two major rockfall accidents in recent years in the North Tower area, one resulting in an amputation. Tourists pose a hazard as well, so be aware that they are above you. A helmet provides some peace of mind.

The rock at Palisade Head tends to be more flaky and brittle than at Shovel Point. This has important consequences for lead climbing. Unexpected loose rock is more likely at Palisade Head than anywhere else described in this guide, and apparently solid protection can pull out (via rock disintegration) even under body weight. Trees have shallow root systems, so consider your anchor choices carefully.

Fixed pins can be found protecting some moves. These pins are likely quite old and have been subjected to much freeze-thaw action. Test pins as thoroughly as possible before clipping to them—but don't ever commit solely to them. The rock doesn't accept stoppers all that well, and you might expect to find some runouts as a result. First-time visitors are strongly urged to consider toproping a few routes or leading climbs well within their abilities. A good selection of protection for wide cracks is required for many of the climbs.

Padding the sharp edges of the rock is absolutely essential. Take along a couple of pieces of thick carpet with keeper loops attached and pad the top edge (and all other danger spots) carefully. Leaders might wish to carry a roll of duct tape to temporarily tape edges. Be especially careful of sharp edges on roofs or flakes. A beefy 11mm rope provides some peace of mind as well. This rock has very sharp crystals that are not always obvious to the naked eye.

The Minnesota Climbing Management Plan: *Climber registration*—Rock climbing permits will be valid for the calendar year and may be obtained free of charge, in person or by mail, by contacting the park office.

Closures—Climbing is generally allowed within the areas at Palisade Head as described in this guide. New route development within this area is allowed within this policy without further permission as long as no additional fixed anchors are needed. Climbers interested in climbing or developing routes outside of these areas or in other parts of the park may request permission in writing through the park manager. Requests for new routes will be reviewed to determine the appropriateness of the request and the impact on park resources.

Seasonal closures of selected areas at Palisade Head to protect nesting peregrine falcons will be in effect from early April through early August. The areas and exact dates will be determined and signed or provided in written materials available to climbers each season, based on the site chosen by the nesting birds. Peregrine falcons are federally endangered and disturbing their nesting areas is punishable under federal law.

Alteration of the Natural Environment—The local climbing ethic at Tettegouche State Park has strongly discouraged the use of chalk. Park Management supports this ethic and encourages climbers to support it also.

Environmental concerns: Palisade Head is home to both peregrine falcons and bats. The falcons have generally been nesting at the far northern end of the cliff, well past *The Poseidon Adventure*, and in most years do not seriously influence the climbing scene. Falcons generally choose a nest site in April and occupy it until August. The area around each nest site is closed to all humans,

NO CHALK AREA

and the closure is marked along the clifftop. If the falcons decide to move their nests south along the cliff (or if more falcons immigrate), some of the climbs described here may be closed for most of the climbing season.

Several species of bats overwinter in the caves and crevices at the base of Palisade Head. The survival of these groups of bats is endangered if they are disturbed while hibernating. It is critical that humans avoid all contact with these caves from mid-fall to mid-spring. Even a quick peek with a flashlight might cause enough disruption to kill the bats weeks later.

Services: State park, state forest, and private campgrounds are all found nearby. Tettegouche State Park is busy all summer, and reservations are necessary (see Appendix A). Two state forest campgrounds are found on Minnesota Highway 1. Eckbeck Campground lies midway between Finland and MN 61 on the Baptism River. Finland Campground lies in the town of Finland. These campgrounds are patrolled, and the camping fees do need to be paid ($9 per night in 1999). Groceries and gasoline are available in Finland (closed evenings) and Silver Bay. Restaurants can be found in Finland, Silver Bay, and Beaver Bay. The Trestle Inn offers a fun dining experience due mainly to its remote location. Our Place (in Finland) serves breakfast at a reasonable price. See Appendix A for more information.

There are no restroom facilities at Palisade Head. Lots of people are tromping around, so choose your site with discretion in mind. Consider bagging and carrying out all solid waste and disposing of it properly.

Approach: (See map in the North Shore introduction.) The logical starting point for all climbs is the parking lot atop the cliff, reached by a sinuous paved road that begins just east of Palisade Baptist Church. The turnoff is 2.8 miles northeast of the stoplight on MN 61 in Silver Bay. This road is gated and locked from 10 P.M. until 8 A.M. Early risers may park in the lot below the gate and walk up (10 minutes). The gate is always locked during the winter (much to the chagrin of the local towing concession). While the cliff actually faces southeast, directions are given as north (toward Shovel Point) and south (toward Silver Bay).

The cliff is logically divided into several sections. Directly below the parking lot is an indentation known as The Amphitheater. From the tourist retaining wall at the southern edge of The Amphitheater, the Southern Ramparts stretches south to *Southern Escape Gully*. South of that you find The South Annex. From the northern edge of The Amphitheater (*Superior Crack*), a large, forbidding wall (The Central Ramparts) runs north, decreasing in height to North Tower. The cliffs past North Tower are shorter, then begin to grow again until the end of the talus at *The Poseidon Adventure*. This area is called the Northern Ramparts.

Traversing the talus below the cliff is easy in good weather, except for one stretch below the south edge of The Amphitheater. A boulder cave provides some climbing that is low fifth class, and using a rope here is a good idea if you don't have the moves wired. Again, remember that rain, ice, wind, and waves can make the talus impassable.

Access to the bases of the climbs depends on your goals. If you are top-roping, either rappelling or lowering down from above is often the simplest solution. Even a longish climb like *Danger High Voltage* can be (barely) top-roped from above. To climb *Danger High Voltage* and more southerly routes from the talus, a descent of *Southern Escape Gully* is the easiest approach. Rappelling into The Amphitheater is the best approach for routes from *Dirty Harry* to North Tower. *Bluebells* is an 80-foot rappel (and a popular climb; avoid leaving an unattended rope). Reach the talus north of North Tower by rappelling in the vicinity of *Arms Race*, *V-Max*, or *Water Babies* (80'). A 60-meter rope makes life more comfortable.

LACERATION JAM—TOP

MABLEY'S TRAVERSE—TOP

NO CHALK AREA

JIM'S CRACK—TOP

DANGER HIGH VOLTAGE—TOP

URGE TO MATE—
TOP

THE BUMP ON THE HEAD

This protuberance is found by walking south to the top of *Laceration Jam* and looking inland. Approach from the right (no photo).

1. **Phrenology** (5.11c) ★ Up and left to an undercling, then up and slightly right. FA: Dave Pagel.

2. **The Noggin** (5.10c) ★ Find a light corner beneath an overhang about half-way up. FA: Dave Pagel.

THE SOUTH ANNEX

Traversing past the top of *Southern Escape Gully*, continue working south. An access gully gets you down to the beach. This is a nice, sheltered spot on cool days; too bad there's only one decent climb here. Lots of loose junk to play with, too.

3. **A Long Night's Journey into Day** (5.7) Up chimney right of free-standing pillar. FA: Rick Kollath.

4. **Genetically Correct** (5.10b) ★★ Up the corner, continuously. Worth doing. FA: Brian Gitar.

5. **M*A*S*H*** (5.6) A right-facing corner. FA: Rick Kollath.

6. **Swimsuits and Harnesses** (5.10) Up through junky cracks just off the right edge of the photo. FA: Dave Pagel.

SOUTH ANNEX

NO CHALK AREA

LACERATION
JAM AREA

THE SOUTHERN RAMPARTS

The main cliff starts at the south end with a rotten gully and extends north to The Amphitheater. This area of the cliff is somewhat more solid than the northern half of the cliff. It is the home to most of the multi-pitch free climbs in the region as well. Most of the routes can be set up as top-ropes. If you are leading, the bottoms of climbs from *Danger High Voltage* south are best reached via the *Southern Escape Gully*.

7. **Southern Escape Gully** (5.0) The easiest way to the bases of the climbs south of The Amphitheater. From the parking lot, hike south along the clifftop. After about 500 feet an obvious loose chute is encountered. Instead of descending here, go a few feet farther south (a bit right) and down a cleaner gully. Eventually reach a badly eroded, very loose trough and rappel (or downclimb). Leaving a fixed line is not a bad idea.

8. **KGB** (5.7) ★ The first major corner right of *Southern Escape Gully* has a large flake in it. The climbing is decent, but the loose gravel at the top is quite annoying. FA: Dave Pagel.

9. **Night Vision** (5.12a) Right of *KGB*, a thin crack in the corner. FA: Steve Mankenberg.

10. **Flight School** (5.10d) ★ Look for a thin seam in the middle of the face. Near the top, move right toward the corner.

11. **Socket Wrench** (5.8) ★ Up the corner. FA: Dave Pagel.

12. **Old Men in Tight Pants** (5.10a) ★ The crack right of the previous climb. FA: Rick Kollath.

NO CHALK AREA

13. **Presents** (5.11a) ★★ Thin, technical, and aesthetic. Start in the small corner/crack just left of *Laceration Jam* and climb up, then right to the first belay on *Laceration Jam*. FA: Dave Pagel.

14. **Christmas Tree Crack** (5.10a) ★★ A little bit of loose rock, but still a nice climb. After the first pitch of *Laceration Jam*, slink left and up this crack. This can be top-roped in conjunction with the first pitch of *Laceration Jam*.

15. **Laceration Jam** (5.10b) ★★ A sustained and well-named climb. Begin in the distinct, curving, hand crack with a tree at its base. **Pitch 1:** The crux pitch leads up the crack, past the overhang, to an airy stance on the left (sling belay). **Pitch 2:** Continue up and traverse right around the corner to a ledge. **Pitch 3:** Climb through an overhang (5.8) and up a chimney (5.6R) to the top. Pro for wide cracks is useful. FA: Jim Kennedy and Dave Mital.

16. **Queen of Venus** (5.10b) A loose flake and crack system just right of *Laceration Jam*. See the next route. FA: Bob Rossi.

17. **Killing Me Softly** (5.11b) ★★ This can be top-roped by gaining the *Laceration Jam* traverse. Right of *Laceration Jam* is a small, right-facing corner (a larger corner farther right is not the route). Climb this to the second belay of *Laceration Jam*. FA: Dave Pagel and Rick Kollath.

18. **Pussyfoot** (5.9) ★★ You get a bit of everything on this route: hands, fists, offwidth, and a roof thrown in for good measure. About 30' north of the previous climb, locate a small pentagonal roof about 40' up. A small tree marks the start, an offwidth section that turns to hands. Above the 5.9 roof, follow the hand crack to a belay at its top. Climb left and up the final chimney on *Laceration Jam*. FA: Rick Kollath and Dave Pagel.

19. **Squab** (5.7) A moderate route that is best left alone due to bad rock.

20. **Scars and Tripes Forever** (5.10a) ★★★ A long, forbidding, dark corner forms the first major break in the clifftop to the north of *Laceration Jam*. Your mission is to reach that corner and climb it. Start about 10' north of a right-facing corner and work up to a small bush. Forge boldly past a wide section (5.9) to the continuously difficult crack above. FA: Dave Pagel.

21. **Mabley's Traverse** (5.8) Dave Pagel's description is the best: "This climb has been compared to the original 1938 route on the Eiger North Face in that it is devious, follows a classic line of weakness, and is littered with dead bodies (mostly pigeons)." Make a rising traverse right along a set of broken ledges. Eventually you do a bit of 5.8 offwidth just below the top, if you are foolish enough to have gone that far. FA: Steve Mabley.

22. **Bridges over Troubled Water** (5.10a) ★ From the *Mabley's Traverse* ledge, make some 5.8 moves up to a fist crack and up to the dihedral, finishing either right or left. FA: Rick Kollath.

NO CHALK AREA

23. **Every which Way but Up** (5.11c) ★★ Right of the cave just north of the *Mabley's Traverse* start is a finger crack that looks easier than it is. Top-rope from the ledge. FA: John Hoivik and Dave Pagel.

24. **Iron Maiden** (5.11a) ★ At least one person has liked this climb, though the torture never stops. Up wide cracks, etc., on the right side of the inset. FA: Dave Pagel.

25. **Swizzlestick Legs** (5.11c) ★ The face (possible bolts) left of *Smearjob*. FA: Chris Holbeck.

26. **Smearjob** (5.10c) ★ The quality is inversely proportional to the amount of mud and dirt in it. FA: Steve Mabley.

27. **Jim's Crack** (5.10a) ★ The crux involves switching sides in an offwidth. FA: Jim Ronnigen, Steve Mabley, and Rick Kollath.

28. **Cul-de-sac** (5.10c) The next crack right of *Jim's Crack*. FA: Rick Kollath.

29. **Yellow Feather** (5.11d+) Thin stemming to easier ground. FA: Rick Kollath.

30. **The Road to Emerald City** (5.12) ★★★ An old aid route, with the first pitch now free on top-rope. The second pitch has apparently been led free. The aid bolts on the first pitch are pretty dicey. FA: Rick Kollath and Dave Pagel(A4); FFA, p.1:Mike Dahlberg (TR).

31. **A Mind Forever Voyaging** (A4) ★★★ Still aid, as far as I know. FA: Dave Pagel and Rick Kollath.

32. **Danger High Voltage** (5.8) ★★★ Prospective leaders should have a thorough grounding in crack technique. This route follows the flake system just north of the lightning cables for the transmission tower. **Pitch 1:** Start right of the cables and improvise your way up into the offwidth crack (you may have to face the water to do this). Belay at the ledge. **Pitch 2:** Work up and right of the flake to the top. Or, a 5.9+ variation requires climbing the offwidth to the left of the final flake. Needless to say, avoid this route in bad weather and take pro for wide cracks. FA: Steve Mabley and Rick Kollath.

33. **A Feathery Tong** (5.10d) ★★ The best approach is from above. A few yards north of the top of Route 32 is a pointed orange rock right on the edge. Rappel down to a ledge to start. The climbing is mostly on steep edges. FA: Chris Holbeck.

THE AMPHITHEATER

A number of good routes are clustered near the parking lot—how convenient! *Bluebells* and *Quetico Crack* can be top-roped from below on a 50-meter rope; other routes must be belayed from above or led. Avoid leaving a fixed line on the main climbs in The Amphitheater.

AMPHITHEATER—LEFT

34. **Dirty Harry** (5.7) ★ This is the best escape route from The Amphitheater area. From the southern corner of The Amphitheater, an obvious line of ledges ascends up and left. Access to these ledges is barred by a corner topped by an overhang. Ascend the corner (5.7), belay, and scramble up the 4th-class ledges to the top.

35. **Sudden Impact** (5.11d) ★★ If the contrived crux moves at the top are avoided, the route is somewhat easier (11b). From the belay ledge at the top of the *Dirty Harry* dihedral, paw your way up the shallow corner above. The crux moves are a few feet below the top, just left of the *Ex Nihilo* finish. FA: Dave Pagel.

36. **Ex Nihilo** (5.10b) ★★★ Climb the large dihedral (5.7) immediately north of the *Dirty Harry* start and belay. The right-facing corner and cracks above form the crux pitch. FA: Rick Kollath.

37. **The Fool's Progress** (5.11) Start in the corner between the next and previous route and follow the bolts.

38. **Rapprochement** (5.10b) ★★★ A reachy crux near the bottom leads to slightly easier climbing above. Start on the face between *Ex Nihilo* and *Sunny and Sheer*. Climb up through double cracklets (crux at pin) and enter the 5.9 corner above.

39. **Sunny and Sheer** (5.12a) ★★ The beat goes on. The arete that marks the southern boundary of The Amphitheater is continuous and strenuous. Start on the left side, traverse right about a third of the way up, and then it gets hard. FA: Eric Fazio-Ricard.

NO CHALK AREA

Bruce McDonald on Phantom Crack. PHOTO: MCDONALD COLLECTION

40. **Palace-Aid** (5.12b) ★★★ Great face climbing on sound rock. Up seams to the left of *Hidden Treasure*. FA: Rick Kollath(A3+); FFA(no falls): Dave Groth.

41. **Hidden Treasure** (5.11b) ★★ No secrets here. The major corner right of *Sunny and Sheer* runs the full height of the cliff and is overhanging most of the way up. Stemming might be a good approach. FA: Jim Kennedy.

42. **Phantom Crack** (5.9) ★★★ The top of this fine climb is often haunted by tourists, so try to smile as the crack gets harder and harder. Just right of *Hidden Treasure* is a lower-angle area leading to another corner. Scamper up the slabs (5.6, limited protection) and climb the hand crack above.

43. **Phantom Corner** (5.12-) Up the corner to the right of *Phantom Crack*. FA: Brian Gitar.

44. **Bluebells** (5.9) ★★★ The better your technique, the easier this 80-foot climb will seem. Jam your way up the marvelous finger crack in the right-facing dihedral in the upper left corner of The Amphitheater. FA: Dick Wildberger and Dan Kieffaber.

45. **Warrior's Last Dance on Earth** (5.12a) This route and the next two lie on the back wall of The Amphitheater, just right of *Bluebells*. This is the left line, which goes up through an overhang partway up. FA: Steve Mankenberg.

46. **Name Unknown** (5.11) Between the surrounding routes. The bolts are gone, so top-rope it.

47. **Gift of the Magi** (5.11d) ★ Start in a corner and trend up and right, finishing closer to *Quetico Crack*. FA: Roger Harkess.

48. **Quetico Crack** (5.8-) ★★ Ask Jesse for advice on the proper technique here (a sleeper hold is useful in one spot). Rassle your way up the chimney and flake system just left of *Superior Crack*.

49. **Superior Crack** (5.8+) ★ This climb may elicit more cursing per linear foot than any other route in this guide. The *Bluebells* corner is paired with a wide crack/corner on the north edge of The Amphitheater. It is harder down low; prepare for a big swing if you fall out.

THE CENTRAL RAMPARTS

The rock from here north becomes progressively worse. Efforts to do free leads of the old aid routes will continue to be stymied by the crumbly rock. The area around North Tower is particularly nasty and has a habit of spitting off large blocks (sometimes with climbers attached).

50. **Wise Guy** (5.12a) ★ The aid variation veers right to a ledge, while the free variation climbs straight up. Hasn't been led free. FA: Rick Kollath(A4-); FFA (TR): Mike Dahlberg.

CENTRAL RAMPARTS

NORTH TOWER

51. **Driving in Duluth** (5.11b) ★★★ A surprisingly moderate tour through some rather featureless terrain. The crux is brief, though some 5.10 moves are sprinkled throughout. The route starts in a vague corner about 30 yards north of *Superior Crack*. Begin from a talus block and weave your way upward. FA: Rick Kollath.

52. **Queen of the Damned** (A3+) ★★ Rotten, no clean ascent yet. 2 pitches FA: Rick Kollath.

53. **Attention Wanders** (5.9) Climb the hand crack to the first belay of Route 54.

54. **A Hard Rain** (A3+) **Pitch 1:** climb shallow corners to a belay (old bolts) beneath a left-facing corner capped by a roof (40'). **Pitch 2:** Up the corner and through the roof, eventually trending right to the belay ledge on Route 55 (150'). **Pitch 3:** Up a thin crack just right of Route 55 (40'). FA: Rick Kollath and Roger Harkess.

55. **Urge to Mate** (5.10c) ★★★ A short but excellent, thin hand crack with good rests and the requisite manky pin at the crux. From the ledge, follow the obvious crack straight up to a crux near the top. FA: Chris Holbeck.

56. **Double-Breasted Anchor** (5.8) ★ A somewhat wide, hanging crack. From the starting ledge, work up, right, and up. FA: Chris Holbeck.

57. **The Great Bird Chimney** (5.7) ★ Obvious from the North Tower area.

58. **Haulbags Are People Too** (5.10d) Up to the base of *The Great Bird Chimney*, cut right up a seam and corner. FA: Rick Kollath and Bill Gitar.

NO CHALK AREA

59. **Comrades in Slings** (A3) ★ The corner left of Route 60. Free it. FA: Rick Kollath.

60. **Mr. Lean** (5.11d) ★★★ The round buttress ends at a tree 20' from the top. A thin crack runs up the north side of the buttress to the tree. FA: Dave Rohne.

61. **Mack the Knife** (5.10b) ★★★ But there aren't any sharks in Lake Superior. North of *Mr. Lean* is an acute corner with a tree and a block at its base. Reach the tree via broken ground to the right. Forge up the corner and be sure to do the final crack moves. FA: Rick Kollath.

62. **Northern Escape Chimney** (5.8) Your best escape from the jaws of destruction if you are north of The Amphitheater. Otherwise, stay away. A short 5.8 section leads to 3rd-class scrambling (loose) to the notch behind North Tower. You may avoid the hard bit by climbing toward the tree on *Mack the Knife*, traversing right, and downclimbing to a lower ledge.

THE NORTHERN RAMPARTS

From North Tower, the cliff drops down, and the trail moves away from the cliff edge. For climbs in the vicinity of *Arms Race*, spot a grove of tall birches while you are at North Tower. Go to that grove, find an eroded area near the cliff edge, and pick a good spot for an 80-foot rappel. Otherwise, pick the cleanest looking area and fix a line (more than 80 feet most other areas).

63. **North Tower, South Face** (5.10d) ★ For safety's sake, just do the final headwall.

64. **Faith** (A3+) ★ Seams on the east face. FA: Dave Pagel and Rick Kollath.

65. **Knife Guys Finish First** (A3) More aid that needs to go free/clean. Climb the seams splitting the north face of the tower. FA: Rick Kollath and Dave Pagel.

66. **Withering Heights** (5.11a) The offwidth on the north side of the tower, watch for loose stuff. FA: Rick Kollath.

67. **Whodunit** (5.9+) Up a ramp to the crux, loose at the top.

68. **Sunday Excursion** (A3) Up corner to triangular overhang, keep going. Pagel took a 90-footer on this route. FA: Dave Pagel.

69. **Keystone** (A3/5.12?) Right of *Sunday Excursion*, now mostly or all free. Chimney to corner to big jammed block. FA: Rick Kollath and Roger Harkess.

70. **Feces Mortibus** (5.10a) Right of pillar to crack, up to ledge and handcrack. FA: Rick Kollath and Bob Bickford.

71. **Bearded Cabbage** (5.11a) Up left of wide crack to thin seams. FA: Brian Gitar.

72. **Arms Race** (5.11c) ★★★ Well named. Below the eroded area is a smooth crack about 10' left of a prominent corner (*Goliath's Finger Crack*). A small ledge a few feet up positions you for the crux. FA: Dave Pagel.

73. **Grey Expectations** (5.11a) Loose and dirty, it's just left of Route 74.

74. **Goliath's Finger Crack** (5.9+) ★ Can you say offwidth technique? I knew you could. The major wide crack in the corner right of *Arms Race*. FA: Bob Bickford.

75. **A Moveable Piece** (5.9) ★ Right of *Goliath's Finger Crack* is an arete that becomes broken at the top. Just north of this arete is a flake. Climb the thin crack up the left side of this flake and cut right to a bush near the top. Dirty from lack of use. FA: Brian Gitar.

76. **In the Wash** (5.9) Up flake, cut a bit right below trees and up. FA: Brian Gitar.

77. **V-Max** (5.11c) This route begins 30' left of *Water Babies* as an acute dihedral with a small cedar about 20' up. FA: Rick Kollath.

78. **Water Babies** (5.8) ★ Just left of a large left-facing corner (the next route) is a smaller corner with a birch halfway up. FA: Brian Gitar and Bill Gitar.

79. **I Could've Been a Contender** (5.8) ★ Loose. A crack on the right wall of the large corner. FA: Dave Pagel.

NORTHERN RAMPARTS—LEFT

NORTHERN RAMPARTS—RIGHT

Hanging
Belay

NORTHERN RAMPARTS—RIGHT

90

92

96

80. **Mohammed Ali** (5.12) ★ Start Routes 80–84 from a brushy ledge just right of the large corner. This route is the face to the right of Route 79. Start on the pedestal, then move left. FA: Mike Dahlberg.

81. **Hidden Agenda** (5.9) ★ Up the hand crack. Very loose at top; it is not known if the bolts below the rim are still good. Not a good top-rope. FA: Rick Kollath.

82. **The Sound of One Hand Jamming** (5.10d) From the right edge of the ledge, up the flake and corner. FA: Rick Kollath and Roger Harkess.

83. **Praise the Many Seraphim** (5.8) ★ Wander up the bolted face right of Route 82. The easiest exit is up and right. FA: Rick Kollath.

84. **Ecclesiastes 1** (5.12a) ★★ A finger crack splits the face right of the ledge. FA: Paul Bjork.

85. **The Last Gift of a Sinner** (5.12b) The next crack right of Route 84. FA: Jeremy Dyer, 1997.

86. **The Metamorphosis** (5.10b) ★ Who knows what you'll find. Definitely loose rock. Big loose rocks.

87. **Soli Deo Gloria** (5.12c) ★ Up the left side of the fairly featureless wall. FA: Paul Bjork.

88. **The Choice of a New Generation** (5.11d) ★★★ A few feet right of the previous route, locate a very thin crack that mutates into a small, right facing corner. FA: Dave Pagel.

89. **No Sugar, No Baby** (5.9) At the last trees along the talus, find a low-angle jamcrack. FA: Rick Kollath.

Note that free climbing efforts have led to a variety of possible routes through the roofs at the far north end of the talus. The descriptions of Routes 90–93 indicate some of the possibilities, but I have no information on the current state of any fixed protection or belay anchors on these routes.

90. **Mital's Roof** (A3) ★★ **Pitch 1:** Over the roof to a bolt station. **Pitch 2:** Easy aid, or free (5.11c). FA: Dave Mital.

91. **The Fall of Ascomytes** (5.12+) **Pitch 1:** Start right of the previous route and join it at the bolt station. **Pitch 2:** The same as the previous route. FA: Rick Kollath.

92. **The Sound and the Fury** (5.12) ★ **Pitch 1:** Locate a large roof with a white patch beneath, near the end of the talus. Climb up and left through roofs to a belay bolt at the end of this roof. **Pitch 2:** Up past some bolts.

93. **Aching Alms** (5.12a/b) ★ Starting right of Route 92, follow a crack through a roof to a rappel station. FA: Seth Schlick, 1997.

NO CHALK AREA

94. **Echoes** (5.11b) ★★ Up a line of bolts just left of the *Poseidon Adventure* start.

95. **Abandoned Child** (5.12+) ★ Continues directly above *Echoes*, no bolts (so top-rope it).

96. **The Poseidon Adventure** (5.11d) ★★★ You will feel the effects of this overhanging corner the morning after. At the end of the talus lives a long, shallow corner. Climb up the lower corner (right of some bolts), step right, then continue up the sustained dihedral above. FA: Dave Pagel and Rick Kollath.

Bruce McDonald on Out on a Limb, *Shovel Point.*

NO CHALK AREA

Shovel Point

The waves were breaking at Robertson's feet and the seal began to bob
up and down in excited anticipation of two new playmates. In these
situations I usually climb well.

—Tom Patey, *The Old Man of Stoer*

Shovel Point is the kinder and gentler of the two waterfront cliffs. The routes
are, unfortunately, shorter than you might think, as the lower part of the cliff is
rather loose. The rock is less steep than most other cliffs in this guide and the
opportunity arises for a different style of climbing as a result. Don't worry,
there are still enough harder routes here to keep you busy.

The big problem is that there are few routes here for the number of climbers
visiting the area. There are several truly moderate routes here that are con-
stantly occupied by guided groups. You will also have the company of many,
many non-climbers who visit the area. This is one of the most popular stops
along the North Shore, and for good reason—the views are tremendous.

Emergency contact: Call 911 or contact the park office. The nearest phone
is at the Tettegouche Rest Area. For campers, there is one pay phone in Finland,
on the south side of the grocery store. Report all accidents to the park office.

The climbing environment: This is a no-chalk area; please read the chalk
ethic information on page 192. Almost all climbs must be approached from
above. Unless you are very sure of your abilities, leave your rappel line in place
as an escape route.

Fixed pins can be found protecting some moves. These pins are likely quite
old and have been subjected to much freeze-thaw action. Test pins as thoroughly as possible before clipping to them—but don't ever commit solely to
them. The rock doesn't accept stoppers all that well, and you might expect to
find some runouts as a result. First time visitors are strongly urged to consider
toproping a few routes or leading climbs well within their abilities. A good
selection of protection for wide cracks is required for many of the climbs.

An obvious hazard is the gravelly, sloping cliff edge. There is some loose
rock, but most of the climbs have been cleaned up. The main hazard would be
getting stuck on a climb; the only way out is up in most cases. Prussik loops or
ascenders can solve this problem if you know how to use them.

Padding the sharp edges of the rock is absolutely essential. Take along a
couple of pieces of thick carpet with keeper loops attached and pad the top

edge (and all other danger spots) carefully. Leaders might wish to carry a roll of duct tape to temporarily tape edges. Be especially careful of sharp edges on roofs or flakes. A beefy 11mm rope provides some peace of mind as well. This rock has very sharp crystals that are not always obvious to the naked eye. Very, very little force is needed to cut a rope under tension.

The Minnesota Climbing Management Plan: *Climber Registration*—Rock climbing permits will be valid for the calendar year and may be obtained free of charge, in person or by mail, by contacting the park office.

Closures—Climbing is generally allowed within the area of Shovel Point described in this guidebook. New route development within the areas described here is allowed within this policy without further permission as long as no additional fixed anchors are needed. Climbers interested in climbing or developing routes outside of these areas or in other parts of the park may request permission in writing through the park manager. Requests for new routes will be reviewed to determine the appropriateness of the request and the impact on park resources.

Alteration of the Natural Environment—The local climbing ethic at Tettegouche State Park has strongly discouraged the use of chalk. Park Management supports this ethic and encourages climbers to support it also.

Environmental concerns: The clifftop is visited by over 100,000 people per year, and the vegetation is being severely trampled along the cliff edge. Changes are planned that will help reverse the damage while at the same time preserving access to climbing. Some of these changes have already begun; others are in the planning stages and may yet be modified. I'll provide an overview of the issues and the proposed solutions.

As of fall 1999, a wooden platform is being constructed near The Great Yawn. This platform (along with others in the planning stage) is designed to limit damage to vegetation and soils by climbers, especially those in groups. By leaving your tarps at home and using these platforms, climbers will help prevent future closures for habitat regeneration.

Two other changes are planned. The trail system along the top will be clarified and a limited number of trails will be kept open along the cliff edge zone. Portions of the cliff edge may be closed to foot traffic; no climbs should be affected, but climbers will need to walk along the main trail and then cut back to the cliff edge to access some routes. The hope is to allow revegetation to occur in some areas without affecting access to climbs.

Finally, anchor bolts will likely be placed at the tops of many of the popular climbs. Climbers are killing the trees along the cliff edge by trampling soil around the bases of trees and by breaking off branches when using the trees as anchors. Loss of trees is the major cause of soil erosion and death of the understory vegetation, and this is the major threat to future access in this area. By providing bolts, the hope is to slow down or stop the loss of trees. Until the bolts are placed at your climb, use trees very carefully. If you must use a tree, approach it by walking on exposed roots and by not removing living or dead wood. Abrasion of the bark is less a problem than damage to the soil beneath the tree–but still don't pull slings and rope around trees.

The park management is committed to maintaining both the natural habitat and access to climbing. Climbers need to do their part by cooperating with the park to make these changes work. You can also help to educate the general public, which is responsible for much of the actual damage.

Approach: (See map in the North Shore introduction.) The approach to Shovel Point begins at the rest area at the entrance to Tettegouche State Park, 4.3 miles northeast of the stoplight at Silver Bay on Minnesota Highway 61. The best spot to park is the far-right (southwest) corner of the lot. Please do not park in the truck area to the left (trail reroutes have made the right lot closer). From the parking area, hike toward the lake and intercept the well-signed path to Shovel Point.

Viewpoints along this trail can be used to help locate the climbs. After climbing a long set of wooden steps, one emerges onto an observation platform. This platform serves as a starting point for locating the climbs. The cliff faces slightly west of south; directions are given as east (toward the end of Shovel Point) and west (toward the parking lot). Cliff edge photos are provided to help locate the general area of your climb.

A number of routes actually start from the talus that can be seen below the observation platform area. These pitches are generally not climbed, so all access descriptions refer to the top of each climb. Usually, a 40–80-foot rappel will deposit you on a small ledge or tree that marks the bottom of the pitch. Many of the climbs are in dihedrals that offer stemming, jamming, liebacks, and face climbing (often simultaneously).

A climbers' trail parallels the cliff edge and provides access to the climbs; here's a summary. As the trail leaves the observation platform and proceeds east, the cliff top is fairly flat. Climbs from Ross's Crack to A Study in Scarlet are located along this stretch. The trail then descends an eroded slope (possible detour here in the future). Narcoleptic Epic is found at a clump of cedars about a third of the way down this slope. At the base of the slope is Rise over Run. The trail proceeds, first level, then slightly downhill, past a broken section of the cliff with many trees on it (possible closure here and detour onto main trail). About 90 yards past Rise over Run the trail passes a white pine and emerges onto a gravel slope which marks the top of Out on a Limb. The trail descends slightly from this point, passing the large corner of The Great Yawn after another 50 yards. Gold Plated is located about 30 yards farther on, next to a small but distinct ridge crossing the trail.

Remember to pad rock edges carefully to prevent rope damage.

TREE ROUTE—TOP

ROSS'S CRACK—TOP

LEFT OF FAERIES—TOP

NO CHALK AREA

RISE OVER RUN—TOP

THE GREAT YAWN—TOP

SHOVEL POINT—LEFT

NO CHALK AREA

1. **The Tree Route** (5.10a) ★★ From the observation platform, walk west along the cliff edge for about 100 feet. Descend a few feet to a clean platform that juts out toward the lake. The climb ends in the east-facing corner. From the talus, a brushy start leads to a nice thin crack that leads to a nice thin crack that leads to a dying cedar about 50' up. From the cedar, scamper up easier slabs (bolted) to a flake and the corner at the top. Use gear as a directional, not the tree.

2. **Straight, No Chaser** (5.10b) ★ A few feet east of *The Tree Route* is a climb with a few neat moves. Zip up to the shrub right of the tree on the previous climb. Join *The Tree Route*, but finish on the short, thin crack above the flake (5.9). FA: Brian Gitar.

3. **Ego-itis** (5.12a) ★★ **Pitch 1:** Ignore this junk (5.9) and rap to the bolt station under the roof. **Pitch 2:** Turn the roof on hopefully solid blocks (bolts). FA: Rick Kollath.

4. **The Great Barrier Roof** (C3/5.11+) ★★★ For the free version, do it in three pitches. Belay the second pitch at the lip of the roof to avoid a sharp edge. **Pitch 1:** Often wet (80', 5.10+). **Pitch 2:** Turn the roof and belay (5.11+). **Pitch 3:** To the top. Can be aided clean on hooks and small nuts. FA: Dave Pagel; FFA: Mike Dahlberg.

5. **Ross's Crack** (5.10b) ★★★ Don't skate, mate. A corner problem with a couple of crusty old pins above the crux. A few feet east of the observation platform is a distinct, west-facing corner. Start from the tree about 60' down, or do a fairly silly approach pitch from the talus below (5.8). FA: Paul Ross.

6. **Balance of Power** (5.11c) ★★★ You could be seriously overdrawn after completing this strenuous and continuous route. Starting from the ledge at the base of *Ross's Crack*, travel up that route a few feet before cutting up and right underneath an overhang. Forge up the tiny corner above the roof. FA: Dave Pagel.

7. **Did Plato Love Trees?** (5.8) Three pitches. **Pitch 1:** Start at end of the talus and climb up to the base of the *Ross's Crack* dihedral and belay. **Pitch 2:** Traverse up and right, then down and right, and belay below the *Faeries* slab. **Pitch 3:** Finish up left of the slab. FA: Rick Kollath, Dave Mital, and Jim Mital.

8. **Dance of the Sugar-Plump Faeries** (5.7–5.10) ★★★ It's interesting that the lowest-angle section of rock in this guide has some of the best climbing in the state. Forty feet east of *Ross's Crack* is a very clean, low-angle slab. This slab has four separate routes, although they do tend to blur together. From the tree below, you can swing into and up the inside corner (5.7); hip-hop up the thin crack a few feet right of the corner (5.8); samba up the face between the crack and the arete (5.10b/c); or tango up the right edge (5.10d).

SHOVEL POINT—
LEFT DETAIL

9. **Sacred Biscuit** (5.11a) ★★★ Don't bite off more than you can chew. Start just east of the *Faeries* slab at a cedar beneath an overhang. Go left of the first roof, then right of the second to the crux crack. FA: Brian Gitar.

10. **A Study in Scarlet** (5.10b) ★★★ Starting at the same place as the previous route, go right for a slightly less taxing outing. FA: Dave Pagel.

11. **A Dream of White Sheep** (5.9) ★★ The route ends at a rotten indentation 10 feet west of the trees. To experience the 5.9 section, follow the diagonal fault that lies to your left as you lower down from above. Following the natural fall line of the rope is a little easier. Exit right below the top.

12. **Straw House** (5.11b) ★★★ Just west of the *Narcoleptic Epic* dihedral is an outside corner. Cruise up this, cut left to a tree beneath a roof, then pull the roof and stroll to the top. FA: Roger Harkess.

13. **Narcoleptic Epic** (5.11d) ★★★ The local Zamboni driver must come over and polish this sucker on a regular basis. Directly below the trees is a very clean dihedral. Thin stemming is an understatement. FA: Dave Pagel.

14. **Wake Up and Smell the Coffee** (5.9) Escape right from Route 13. FA: Rick Kollath.

15. **Rise over Run** (5.7-) ★★ At the bottom of the gravel slope is a notch with some smallish blocks at the top. A straightforward romp up nice rock.

NO CHALK AREA

SHOVEL POINT—CENTER

SHOVEL POINT—RIGHT

16. **Cornered** (5.9) ★★ Not a bad route. Find a big west-facing corner. There were still owls nearby, last I checked. FA: Dave Mital.

17. **A Touch of Leather and Lace** (5.7) A few feet east of *Cornered*. FA: Raven Corbett.

18. **Out on a Limb** (5.6) ★★ Almost always occupied, and with good reason. From *Rise over Run*, walk east on level, then downsloping ground for about 90 yards. The cliff edge is rounded, loose, and quite vegetated through here. Emerge onto a cleaner gravel slope and locate a poorly defined corner. A bolt can be seen on a slab part of the way down.

19. **Only the Lonely** (5.6) ★★ A little harder and less well-traveled than the other climbs of this grade. A few yards east of *Out on a Limb*, just east of a spruce is a small notch that marks the top. FA: Rick Kollath.

20. **Only the Looney** (5.9) A finger crack leads to a thin traverse left at the top. FA: Rick Kollath.

21. **Soldier of God** (5.5) ★★ A fun little climb, with little being the key word. Halfway between *Out on a Limb* and *The Great Yawn*, locate an unusually clean section of clifftop with a large spruce just below. Descend 30' to the beginning of the climbing. FA: Rick Kollath.

22. **I Laughed, I Cried, It Became a Part of Me** (5.10a) Just east of the next climb. FA: Dave Pagel.

23. **The Great Yawn** (5.6) ★★★ Not a ho-hum route, it has a good deal of decent jamming. About 50 yards past *Out on a Limb* is a large corner with rock "fingers" on the east side (you'll see what I mean). Protection for wide cracks is useful for leading the lower sections.

24. **Undercover** (5.10c) Just west of the previous climb. FA: Dave Pagel and Jim Kennedy.

25. **Gold Plated** (5.10b) ★★★ For full effect, this climb is best done when the lake is angry. About 100' past the previous climb a two-foot ridge crosses the trail. The top of the climb is a small corner near this ridge. From a ledge about 50 feet down, spiral your way up through two roofs and claw your way to the top.

MYSTICAL MOUNTAIN ZONE OVERVIEW

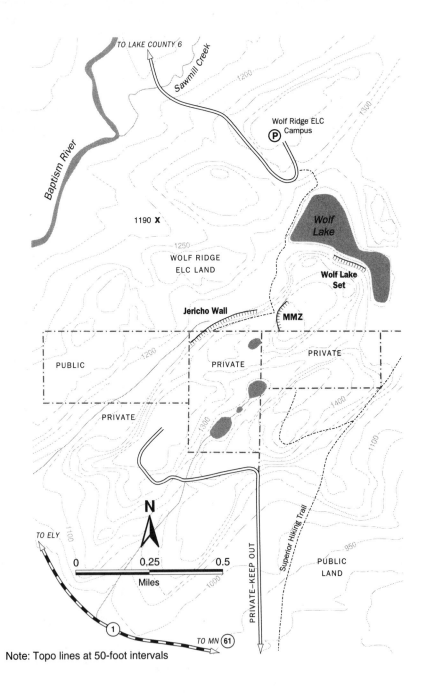

TO LAKE COUNTY 6

Sawmill Creek

1200

1300

Wolf Ridge ELC
P Campus

Baptism River

1190 **X**

Wolf
Lake

1250

WOLF RIDGE
ELC LAND

**Wolf Lake
Set**

Jericho Wall

MMZ

PRIVATE

PUBLIC

1200

PRIVATE

PRIVATE

1400

PRIVATE

1300

1100

N

TO ELY

1100

0   0.25   0.5

Miles

Superior Hiking Trail

PRIVATE–KEEP OUT

950

PUBLIC
LAND

1000

1

TO MN 61

Note: Topo lines at 50-foot intervals

NO CHALK AREA

Mystical Mountain Zone

We are very lucky to be able to climb in an area as wild as the North Shore. The wilderness is disappearing year by year as roads get wider and more and more people buy and build in the region. In the first edition of *Superior Climbs*, Rick Kollath wrote that Johnson [Wolf] Lake "appeals to the climber seeking something beyond the experience of rock climbing . . . a Walden Pond, a quiet respite from the bustling world. . . ." Today, Wolf Lake is part of the bustling world, home to thousands of ten-year-olds every year. The adventurous approaches of yesteryear have been replaced by roads and trails. We should be pleased that the development is being used to teach children about the natural world.

The solitude is almost gone, but the spiritual nature of the area is only quiescent and may still be tapped by those willing to stop and listen. Listen for the slap of a beaver's tail as you approach its dam, and realize that the tiny cedars in the cracks may be hundreds of years old. Study the intricate patterns of moss and lichen on the boulders, and listen for the cry of the falcon. Ask the fifth graders at Wolf Ridge to show you their discoveries, and share in their excitement.

Emergency contact: Call 911 and, if the office is open, inform Wolf Ridge staff. There is a phone at Wolf Ridge, inside the office building. Otherwise, the nearest public phones are in Finland (on the south side of the grocery store), at the Tettegouche Rest Area, and finally in Silver Bay. The nearest hospital is in Two Harbors, about 40 miles west along Minnesota 61.

The climbing environment: Only a small portion of the Mystical Mountain Zone is on public land. The private landowners that allow access to the cliffs have requested that climbers follow a few simple rules in return. The main landowner is the Wolf Ridge Environmental Learning Center (WRELC). Most climbers park in their lot, hike on their trails, and climb on their cliffs. WRELC has been friendly to climbers; please abide by these rules so we can keep it that way.

Wolf Ridge assumes no liability or responsibility for climbers on their property or in the area in general. You are climbing at your own risk. By climbing here, you agree that Wolf Ridge is not liable or responsible for anything that happens to you in this area.

1) Chalk is not to be used on these cliffs.

2) Park only in the visitor's parking area. Cars parked on the road are a hazard to children and will be towed.

3) Each day you climb, check in and check out at the administration building (the first building on your left as you cross the driveway). Any updates on access, trails, or falcon closures will be available here. If the office is closed, leave a note with your name, number in party, and a description of your vehicle.

4) Wolf Ridge will not come looking for you if you fail to check out, but please check out as a courtesy to WRELC.

5) Wolf Ridge is a day-use area; there is no overnight parking or camping on Wolf Ridge property.

6) Please respect the natural environment. Stay on established trails, minimize erosion, and do not litter.

7) Please cooperate with and respect the students and staff of Wolf Ridge.

8) Commercial and other guided groups must consult with the WRELC staff prior to taking groups into the area.

9) Swimming is at your own risk, and the beach is only available for use if no Wolf Ridge students are present.

Services: Camping is available throughout the area. Tettegouche State Park is busy all summer, and reservations are necessary (see Appendix A). Two state forest campgrounds are found on Minnesota Highway 1. Eckbeck Campground lies midway between Finland and Minnesota Highway 61 on the Baptism River. Finland Campground is in the town of Finland. These campgrounds are patrolled, and the camping fees do need to be paid ($9 per night in 1999). Private camping is available, along with motels, cabins, B&Bs, and swank lakeside resorts. See Appendix A for more information.

Groceries and gasoline are available in Finland (closed evenings) and Silver Bay. Restaurants can be found in Finland, Silver Bay, and Beaver Bay. The Trestle Inn offers a fun dining experience due mainly to its remote location on Lake County Road 7, 19 miles from Finland. Our Place (in Finland) serves breakfast at a reasonable price.

Approach: From the town of Little Marais, 60 miles northeast of Duluth on Minnesota Highway 61, go west on Lake County Road 6 for 4.3 miles to the Wolf Ridge road. This road is 2.7 miles south of the intersections of Minnesota Highways 1 and 6 in Finland. Put your car in second gear and drive *slowly* up this 2.5-mile gravel road—there are many elementary school students walking along the last mile of this road. Park only in the visitor's parking area (it's a fairly long walk to the impound lot from here) and check in at the office.

Walk back down the road to the sharp curve about 100 yards down. Turn left on the trail, and follow signs to the Lake Study Area (take every right-hand turn). Staying on the trails is essential for continued access to these crags. Pass by the canoe dock and ignore the side trail to your right. Pass the swimming area and reach the Lake Study Area. Cross the bridge over the stream flowing to your right. This should take about 20 minutes from the car and is all downhill. The approaches to each cliff are described from this point.

WOLF LAKE SET

Formerly known as the Johnson Lake Set, I have renamed this crag to fit with current usage. The crag is obvious, seemingly a short jaunt around the lake from the Lake Study Area. However, one must grovel through cedars and talus to reach it from below. Stay near the lakeshore until you reach the narrow section of the lake, then try to find the cliffs through the trees. The approach gully passes to the right of the main crag and is steep, but passable. If you find yourself doing desperate lunges up collapsing dirt gullies, you're in the wrong place. Another approach would be to climb up and left of Mystical Mountain, go over the ridgetop, and find a faint trail above the cliffs.

There is a falcon nesting box on the cliff. The Wolf Ridge staff will inform you if it's occupied and the cliff is closed.

1. **Crow Crack** (5.9+) Offwidth, probably underrated. FA: Steve Mabley and Jim Ronnigen.

2. **Crow's Nest Traverse** (5.5) Actually, they're ravens and they nest here. Please keep away until mid-June. Escape from the crux of Route 1. FA: Steve Mabley and Jim Ronnigen.

3. **Caw Caw** (5.10b) Ditto on avoiding the ravens. Climb the crack on the face and ooze left. FA: Steve Mabley and Jim Ronnigen.

WOLF LAKE SET—LEFT

4. **Blue-Eyed Delight** (5.8) Go up the left side of an overhang to a fist crack, probably in the company of water. FA: Steve Mabley and Jim Ronnigen.

5. **Two Cent's Worth** (5.7) Avoid the final crack on Route 4. FA: Steve Mabley and Rick Kollath.

6. **Shriek Foot** (5.9) ★ This interesting diversion works up and right of Route 4.

7. **Slippery Razor Spittoon** (5.8) Offwidth. FA: Steve Mabley and Jim Ronnigen.

8. **Physical Negotiation** (5.10c) ★ Up the prow and over the overhang. FA: Jim Blakley.

9. **Greasy Gulch** (5.7) On the right side of the gully find a crack leading to a left-facing corner. FA: Steve Mabley and Jim Ronnigen.

10. **Puddle Paddler** (5.9+) Start below and right of the previous route in a corner leading to vegetation. FA: Steve Mabley.

11. **Up Your Crack** (5.9-) ★★ From the broken ledges halfway up the cliff, climb a black corner/face until you reach the overhang. Work up and right, then up the crack to the top. FA: Steve Mabley and Jim Ronnigen.

12. **Bushwhack Crack** (5.7) Climb a crack near some vegetation. FA: Steve Mabley and Jim Ronnigen.

13. **Pratt Fraternity** (5.6) Escape from *Up Your Crack*. FA: Rick Kollath.

14. **Loose as a Goose** (5.9) ★★ On the southeast face of the West Column. FA: Steve Mabley and Rick Kollath.

WOLF LAKE SET—RIGHT

NO CHALK AREA

The peregrine nest box sits on the face of the column. Birds have nested there twice; please do not disturb the box.

15. **West Column Ramp** (5.5) On the right side of the West Column. FA: Jim Ronnigen.

16. **Sixty-Second Crack** (5.8) ★★ The left wall of the approach gully has a set of disjointed cracks; look up to see them. FA: Steve Mabley and Rick Kollath.

MYSTICAL MOUNTAIN

The most popular crag in this area, it still sees only a fraction of the traffic seen at Palisade Head or Shovel Point. It's also one of the tallest crags in the state. Both sections are about 130 feet tall, so slingshot top-ropes are not feasible on many routes. In some cases a rappel to an intermediate ledge allows a top-rope with bottom belay. Otherwise, belay from the top or lead 'em. A fixed rap line makes life easier, and burly ropes provide peace of mind on the anorthosite. Cams and medium-to-large stoppers work well.

From the Lake Study Area, turn right (following the left side of the stream) and hike down the valley. The trail zigs up and left, soon reaching a large, white boulder. Skirt the boulder to the left and head directly uphill on an eroded trail. Watch for (and follow) any future trail reroute through this area. You will end up at the right end of Mystical Mountain West, beneath *Black Gate* and *Horner's Corner*.

Continue uphill and right around the cliff, past the access gully for the top of Mystical Mountain, to Mystical Mountain South. The trail descends along the base of the rock, around a corner and bends right (near *Mother Goose*) into a pretty grove of cedars. Continued trampling of this area will lead to the death of these trees, so please walk around the margins of this grove.

The cliff is naturally divided into two sections: Mystical Mountain West (the first section one encounters on the approach from below), and Mystical Mountain South (up and right of Mystical Mountain West). Access to the top is via a gully between the two sections. This gully is eroding badly, so please tread lightly. Cut left up a root-laced chimney that usually has a fixed rope (Class 2–3). This puts you above *Black Gate*. To reach the South section, climb up a few feet and reach an obvious trail to the right. The South Section may also be reached from the far right end of the cliff.

MYSTICAL MOUNTAIN WEST

The cliff is about 130 feet tall in its left side. Slingshot top-ropes can be set up on *Jack Be Nimble* and many other routes from midway ledges.

17. **Gollum's Stairwell** (5.9) ★ Just left around the corner from *Jack Be Nimble* is an impressive offwidth. Valley wannabes, go to it. FA: Steve Mabley and Rick Kollath.

MYSTICAL MOUNTAIN
WEST—FAR LEFT

18. **Jack Be Nimble** (5.10a) ★★★ The leftmost climb on the face proper. An acute corner leads to a triangular overhang. Pull the roof (crux) to a ledge and handcracks above. This used to be rated 5.8! FA: Steve Mabley and Rick Kollath.

19. **Fractured Fairy Tail** (5.6) ★★ Climb the jaggedy crack/chimney past a small cedar. If you are smart, finish on the handcrack of *Jack Be Nimble*. If you're not, grunge straight up (5.7). FA: Dan Koch.

20. **Over the Rainbow** (5.7+) ★★★ Right of *Fractured Fairy Tail* is a white, left-facing corner. Lieback the corner, then climb up and right in a thin, mossy crack. Continue up into an A-shaped alcove in the roof. Pull through and climb past two small cedars (be very nice to them, please). FA: Rick Kollath.

21. **Claw Marks of the Cave Bear** (5.10d) ★ Climb the thin face left of the *Hobbit's Demise* corner, then growl up the face between the leftmost pair of cracks on the upper headwall. FA: Rick Kollath.

22. **Hobbit's Demise** (5.10b) ★★ Start up the large, vegetated left-facing corner. Cut left up a steep ramp/corner. Traverse right to the crack right of the *Over the Rainbow* finish. FA: Rick Kollath.

23. **Walking Toto** (5.7) The crack to the right of the *Hobbit's Demise* finish. FA: Brian Gitar.

The next five routes are found on the black, often wet wall to the left of the low roof.

24. **Danse Macabre** (5.11d) ★ Fifteen feet right of the edge of the black face is a small, right-facing corner that mutates into a crack with two small trees. It ends on the midway ledge. FA: Jim Blakley.

25. **Mephisto Waltz** (5.11c) ★★ Twenty feet right of *Danse Macabre* is a thin seam with a pocket about 8' above the sloping ledge at the start. FA: Jim Blakley and Steve Mabley.

26. **Nymphiad** (5.11a) ★ Fourteen feet right of *Mephisto Waltz* is a right-facing corner with a large talus block at its base. Climb up past a bush to the ledge, then continue up the face above. FA: Rick Kollath.

27. **Humpty Dumpty** (5.7) The right side of the black wall degenerates into an ugly, broken corner system. This route supposedly starts at the left end of the overhang that is 7' above the ground. Why you would climb this is an absolute mystery. FA: Steve Mabley and Jim Ronnigen.

28. **Br'er Rabbit** (5.8) At the right end of the overhang is a crack that ends 25' up. Don't bother. FA: Steve Mabley and Jim Ronnigen.

29. **Black Gate** (5.10a) ★★★ In the world of the vertical, how can something so horizontal be so troubling? Twelve feet right of the overhang is a thin crack, just left of a large talus block. Up the crack, traverse slightly left, then up to the top. FA: Steve Mabley.

MYSTICAL MOUNTAIN
WEST—LEFT

30. **Horner's Corner** (5.5) ★ On the right edge of the main face is a low-angle crack with a ledgey area and a cedar at its base. Up this crack to a hanging dihedral. FA: Steve Mabley and Rick Kollath.

MYSTICAL MOUNTAIN SOUTH

From the top of the access gully work up to a defined trail and follow it to the South section. In the vicinity of *Oz Before the Wizard* the cliff is about 130 feet tall, making slingshot top-ropes somewhat problematic. The hard cracks starting from the vegetated ledge can be set up from a lower ledge, reached by rappel.

31. **Surrender Dorothy** (5.11c) ★ Just about where you turn left to climb up and out of the approach gully, look right. A small right-facing corner leads to a seam, and a scraggly pine is directly above. FA: Rick Kollath.

The next 2–3 routes begin from a large, vegetated, but pleasant ledge about 15 feet above the ground.

32. **The Lair of Shelob** (5.12a) ★ A crack 8' left of *Cirith Ungol* deadends 20' up. If you get that far, traverse right and up. FA: Steve Mabley and Jim Blakley.

33. **Cirith Ungol** (5.11c) ★★★ The continuous crack that rises from the ledge. FA: Steve Mabley and Jim Blakley.

34. **Swords of Zanzibar** (5.9) ★★ The ledge ends at a large dead pine. Two cracks start at ground level by this pine—this is the left crack. You can also start this route from the ledge. FA: Steve Mabley and Rick Kollath.

MYSTICAL MOUNTAIN SOUTH— LEFT

35. **Arrows and Slings** (5.11b) ★★ The right-hand crack.

36. **Three Hacks at a Crack** (5.11c) ★★ About 30' right of *Swords of Zanzibar* is a white area of rock. A thin crack starts 10' right of a right-facing corner. Follow the thin crack up, curve right, then cut left (5.9) or right (5.6). FA: Dave Pagel.

37. **Oz Before the Wizard** (5.7) ★★ Continue past *Three Hacks . . .* and around a corner. Start across from a large birch, at cracks directly below a tall pine 30' up. Jam the cracks (5.7) to the pine, ascend a recess to a small ledge, then follow a neat, low-angle finger crack (5.7-) to the top. FA: Rick Kollath.

38. **Mother Goose** (5.5) ★ Twenty feet right of the previous route, a chimney leads to the right end of the pine ledge. Continue up slabs and corners to the top.

39. **Sisyphus** (5.7) ★★ About 30' right of *Mother Goose*, climb up, eventually traversing left to a tree and flake. Do not climb the loose flakes directly below the ledge; start closer to *Old Number Nine*. FA: Steve Mabley and Jim Blakley.

40. **Ode to a Newt** (5.8) The face left of the *Old Number Nine*.

41. **Old Number Nine** (5.7) ★★ A good newbie route. A large boulder leans against the wall. Climb the clean corner to the dead pine, then zip to the top. FA: Rick Kollath and Dan Koch.

MYSTICAL MOUNTAIN
SOUTH—CENTER

MYSTICAL MOUNTAIN
SOUTH—RIGHT

NO CHALK AREA

42. **The Desolation of Smaug** (5.11) Right of the boulder is a short, right-facing corner. Turn the roof to the right and roar up the face, finishing right of the crack. FA: Dave Pagel.

43. **Advice from a Caterpillar** (5.9) Stay right of the previous route, finishing on the 5.9 finger crack. FA: Dave Pagel.

JERICHO WALL

A big, hulking diorite wall, it is large, complex, and loose. It is guarded at the base by a swamp and steep talus; at the top only occasional overlooks allow you to get your bearings. A number of routes have been done here (see *Superior Climbs*). You are on your own. The far-right end (Gunnin' for Glory Buttress) may be on the White Tail Ridge property and would therefore be off-limits to climbing. Other parts may be on private land as well; only a surveyor can decide.

The trail to the top of Jericho Wall leaves the cedar grove of Mystical Mountain South and may be indistinct. Leave the cedar grove at a bearing of 260 degrees, following a shallow scoop or depression. The trail is indistinct here. After 56 feet the trail bends left (230 degrees) for 44 feet and skirts some boulders to the left. Curve right for 40 feet to the base of a small outcrop. Climb easily to the top and hike about 125 feet due southwest through a flat, rather open area. A lookout to your right should reveal a buttress that is part of Jericho Wall. Other lookouts are present on this ridge, but they are not obvious from the trail. To reach the base of the wall, continue down the valley from the white boulder mentioned in the Mystical Mountain approach.

Bruce McDonald on Afghanistan Bananastand, *Sawmill Creek Dome.*

NO CHALK AREA

LAKE COUNTY ROAD 6 AREAS

Two of a kind. Both Section 13 and Sawmill Creek Dome are anorthosite bluffs with excellent views of the valleys below. Both lie 30 to 40 minutes from Lake County Road 6. Both have climbs about 60 feet long. Both can be empty of climbers even on a busy weekend due to the approach hike, which is on the well-traveled Superior Hiking Trail (SHT).

Section 13 offers one of the best inland views on the North Shore. You may be temporarily disappointed on your first visit to find the climbs are so short. That will end as you jam up your first crack; sixty feet seems plenty at that point. Don't miss the slab route, which is completely out of character with the rest of the climbs here.

Sawmill Creek Dome is more forested but still offers good views. The primary attraction to climbers is a few moderate, steep routes and a selection of roof routes at the far end of the cliff. Both areas lie on county land, so be careful of hunters (grouse, deer, etc.) any time after Labor Day. Even if you are on the Superior Trail, wearing orange is advisable.

Emergency contact: Call 911. The nearest public phones are in Finland (on the south side of the grocery store, 5 miles west on County Road 6), at the Tettegouche Rest Area (9 miles east), and finally in Silver Bay. The nearest hospital is in Two Harbors, about 40 miles to the west.

The climbing environment: You are still in the no-chalk ethic zone; review the chalk section (see page 192) in the North Shore introduction if necessary. Cams work well in the rock, as does passive protection. The anorthosite abrades both skin and gear, so make sure you pad your anchor systems appropriately. Tape is useful; you might also appreciate the skin-preserving properties of the rugby shirts and painter's pants worn by climbers of yore.

No fixed gear is found on these crags, and none is needed. Virtually all significant lines follow crack systems. Hunters are following critters in the fall, so wear bright clothing.

Services: Camping is available throughout the area. Tettegouche State Park is busy all summer and reservations are necessary (see Appendix A). Two state forest campgrounds are found on Minnesota Highway 1. Eckbeck Campground lies midway between Finland and MN 61 on the Baptism River. The Finland

LAKE COUNTY ROAD 6 AREAS OVERVIEW

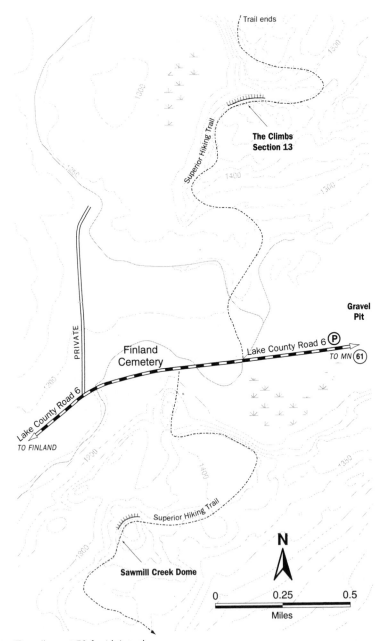

Trail ends

Superior Hiking Trail

**The Climbs
Section 13**

**Gravel
Pit**

Lake County Road 6 Ⓟ

TO MN ⑥①

PRIVATE

**Finland
Cemetery**

Lake County Road 6

TO FINLAND

Superior Hiking Trail

Sawmill Creek Dome

N

0   0.25   0.5

Miles

Note: Topo lines at 50-foot intervals

NO CHALK AREA

Campground lies in the town of Finland. These campgrounds are patrolled, and the camping fees do need to be paid ($9 per night in 1999). Private camping is available, along with motels, cabins, B&Bs, and swank lakeside resorts. See Appendix A for more information.

Groceries and gasoline are available in Finland (closed evenings) and Silver Bay. Restaurants can be found in Finland, Silver Bay, and Beaver Bay. The Trestle Inn offers a fun dining experience due mainly to its remote location. Our Place (in Finland) serves breakfast at a reasonable price.

Approach: Parking for these areas is at the Superior Trail parking lot—an old gravel pit—on Lake County Road 6, 1.1 miles north of MN 61. Do not park on the road or at either trailhead. The eastbound SHT crosses the road 0.1 mile north of the lot; the westbound SHT crosses the road 0.3 mile north of the lot. Note that the eastbound section of the SHT that leads to Section 13 is scheduled for rerouting, though a spur trail to Section 13 will probably remain. Currently, the trail deadends in Section 13 due to access problems.

SAWMILL CREEK DOME

Sawmill Creek Dome is best approached via the Superior Hiking Trail. From the parking lot hike north along the road for 0.3 mile and turn left (west). Gain about 250 vertical feet and reach a ridgeline with views to the north and a small cliff below. The trail then bends southwest to the base of the summit dome, where it climbs steeply to the top. Continue along the trail to a terraced rock overlook with a few large pines. You are now above *Birch Flakes*.

NORTHEAST SECTION

These routes can be found by branching off the Superior Trail at the Picnic Rock sign and scouting them from the base. Routes 6–8 are more easily found by working back from the Central climbs. The first five routes are included for historical purposes only.

1. **Divided We Fall** (5.?) A wide crack through a wide roof.

2. **Here Be Dragons** (5.9?) Handcrack right of an overhang; wet. FA: Dave Pagel.

3. **The Course of Ancient Astronauts** (5.?) "A damp, mossy crack." FA: Dave Pagel.

4. **Road Map** (5.8) A short and fractured wall. FA: Steve Mabley and Jim Blakley.

5. **Legend** (5.6) Offwidth corner, right of the previous route. FA: Steve Mabley and Jim Blakley.

6. **No Rest for the Wicked** (5.11c) ★ Inside corner, often wet. FA: Steve Mabley and Jim Blakley.

EASTERN SECTION

7. **Blueberry Jam** (5.8) Fist crack right of *No Rest for the Wicked*. FA: Steve Mabley and Jim Blakley.

8. **Hummock, Tussock, Stomach** (5.8) Around the corner right of *Blueberry Jam*, right of a Class 4 gully. Right of this is a zone of roofs that ends at *Birch Flakes*.

CENTRAL SECTION

Hike the Superior Trail to a large, terraced overlook. A wooded gully cleaves the cliff; a dark slab may be seen across the gully. The gully is steep in a couple of spots—it's not for children—but is not more than Class 2. A climber's track branches off right of the main trail to descend the gully, but some brush makes the first 30 feet difficult to follow.

9. **Birch Flakes** (5.9) ★★★ This flake/crack system shoots up the left edge of the left wall of the descent gully past a birch. The crux is at the bottom, then easy cruising past the tree to the top. Setup: a notch below the lowest accessible pine. FA: Steve Mabley and Jim Blakley.

10. **The Wonderful World of Huecos** (5.9) ★★★ It's sort of like sticking your fingers into the mouth of a northern pike. Start at the *Julie Gets Flowers* ledge, traverse left and up, then right and up. There is at least one pin left near the top. FA: Rick Kollath.

11. **Julie Gets Flowers** (5.9-) ★★ The right-hand crack line on this face. Start from a ledge 30' above the bottom of the gully. FA: Rick Kollath.

12. Afghanistan Bananastand (5.8) ★★ A huge roof is found just west (right) of the access gully. Climb the inside corner at the left end of the roof (crux) then turn the roof to easier climbing (5.5). The protection is passable on the upper slab. FA: Steve Mabley and Jim Blakley.

WEST SECTION

To approach these climbs, follow the side trail leading to the gully access to the previous routes. Stay left, paralleling the cliff edge, then drop down a few steps and observe another overlook on your right. There are no routes there. Continue in the same direction, following your nose, until you find yourself looking down on a ledge that forms another overlook. Set up your ropes from that ledge. The large V-cleft is the top of *Micropedimorph*. Reach the base by walking farther along the approach trail and down, or by rappelling.

13. A Farewell to Arms (5.11c) ★★★ Left of a 10-foot-high block are two shallow corners; the left one is light green. Climb up this to the saplings and head for the crack/flake in the roof left of *Micropedimorph* (or go straight up). At the roof, count to three and take off. The roof crack to the left awaits an ascent. FA: Steve Mabley and Jim Blakley.

14. Micropedimorph (5.8) ★ Go straight up the black streak to a big notch in the roof. To lead this (not recommended), start from the left side of the flake mentioned above and traverse a long way right to the notch. FA: Steve Mabley.

WEST OVERHANGS—TOP

WEST OVERHANGS—ROOF EXITS

NO CHALK AREA

15. **Once in a While** (5.11d) ★★ To the right of the black streak, a series of roofs runs about 10' above the ground. Just right of the center of this roof system is a lichen-covered seam with a cedar about 20' up. Crack the crux, then scamper up to the roof (5.9). Only minor gardening should be needed. FA: Jim Blakley.

16. **That Hideous Strength** (5.11c) ★ The lower overhang is interrupted by a prow of sorts 8' right of the previous route. Get the juglet on top of this, then fire up and slightly right to the steep, dark face (just right of a minor crack). This and *Bubble Up* can be top-roped from the same setup.

17. **Bubble Up** (5.9) ★★ Don't fizzle out too soon. At the right end of the lower overhangs is a block the size of a 12-pack. Grunt up onto this, then forge straight up (or slightly right) to easier rock not far above. Setup: in a notch just right of a large birch at the left end of the ledge. FA: Pete Holler and Roy McDonald.

SECTION 13

Section 13 is approached from the SHT parking lot on Highway 6 (Lake County Road 6). Walk north a few hundred yards, and turn right on the trail. Do not park here, please. Head north on the trail, first on the flat then climbing. After an initial "summit," descend, pass a spur trail, then make a final climb. The magnificent view signals your arrival at the top of the climbing area. Allow about 30 minutes for the approach. A reroute of the SHT will likely change the signage in the area, though the trail to Section 13 will likely still exist as a spur trail.

Many of the routes start from a narrow ledge about 60 feet from the top of the cliff. Take a couple of 2- to 3-inch cams for anchors at the ledge, or fix a line down to the ledge. The trees on the ledge are barely anchored and are not safe belay anchors. Belaying from above is probably more comfortable in most cases if you are top-roping.

18. **Junk Culture** (5.8) Follow a crack left of *Reading Braille*. FA: Charles Bernick and Rick Kollath.

19. **Reading Braille** (5.11b) ★★★ Follow a thin crack, then leave the crack when it trends right. The wider crack is out of bounds.

20. **The Path of Fierce Black Wolves** (5.10a) ★★ Follow the dike. FA: Rick Kollath.

21. **In Limbo** (5.10d) ★★★ Start up the left side of a flake, then face-climb, staying right of the previous route.

22. **In the Valley** (5.10d) ★★★ Do the right side of the flake and traverse right to a thin crack. FA: Steve Mankenberg.

SECTION 13—TOP RIGHT

SECTION 13—TOP LEFT

NO CHALK AREA

OVERVIEW

SECTION 13 DETAIL

NO CHALK AREA

23. **Macho Pitchu** (5.9+) ★★ A shallow, yellowish corner is the start of this route and the next. Do the dihedral and zag to the top. FA: Steve Mabley.

24. **Brenda's Last Fling** (5.10c) ★★ Way-honed rock betties start the previous climb, then move right and up to create a more difficult route. FA: Dave Pagel.

25. **Equinox** (5.10a) ★★★ About 20' left of the following climb is a finger-and-hand crack. Crank the crux (the first 15'), then up to a fairly tricky finish in a thin crack. Set a rope at the top of the *Rubble Trouble* ramp to climb *Equinox* and *Arrowhead Left* (but not *Rubble Trouble*). FA: Jim Blakley.

26. **Arrowhead Left** (5.8-) ★ Gain the top of the leaning block. Undercling left and follow a left-facing corner. At the top, follow the ramp left (the top of *Rubble Trouble*) or the thin crack straight up. The finishes you take on these two climbs depend on your setup if top-roping. FA: Jim Blakley.

27. **Lower Slab** (5.8) ★ The slab directly below the leaning block can be top-roped from the ledge. An extra rope and a desire to climb furry rock are all that's needed.

28. **Arrowhead Direct** (5.9-) ★★ Climb the center of the arrowhead on delightful pockets and knobs. FA: Rick Kollath.

29. **Rubble Trouble** (5.7) ★★ Right of the leaning block is a tall, sharp flake. Gain the top via the left side (5.6) or right (5.8), then follow the left-trending corner to a short, thin crack (the top of *Arrowhead Left*), or up the ramp. FA: Rick Kollath.

30. **Rubble Trouble Direct** (5.9) ★★★ A stellar crack that branches off right at the base of the ramp. Go right now and climb it. FA: Steve Mabley.

31. **Digit Damage** (5.11a) ★★★ Start in the "access gully" and work through an overhang, fire a finger crack, articulate left, and fire a second crack. I'm tired just thinking about it. FA: Dave Pagel.

32. **Seam's Hard** (5.11b) ★★ Grind up a small dihedral to yet another thin crack. FA: Dave Pagel.

33. **We Don' Need No Steenkin' Ledges** (5.10a) ★★ An impressive slab provides a unique opportunity for Midwestern climbers.

Bruce McDonald on #16, Carlton Peak.

NO CHALK AREA

CARLTON PEAK

Carlton Peak is the prototypical anorthosite dome on the North Shore. It is the highest point along the shore (over 900 feet above the lake) and it commands a dramatic view from its summit. On top you will find the foundation of a fire tower that was used until the 1950s. Below the peak there is considerable evidence of the quarrying that took place since the turn of the century. The area was owned by the 3M Corporation and was purchased by The Nature Conservancy; it is now part of Temperance River State Park. The Temperance River is so named because of the lack of a bar at its mouth. It's worth hiking along the river to take in the view of the gorge, one of the prettier spots along the North Shore.

The climbs here are typical anorthosite–about 60 to 80 feet long and generally abrasive. The climbs don't have names, so I have preserved the numbering system used in Dave Pagel's *Superior Climbs, 2nd Edition*.

Emergency contact: Dial 911 or contact the park office. The public phone closest to the Britton Peak parking lot is at the grocery store on Minnesota Highway 61. There is also a pay phone in the park office, which is closer to the quarry road approach. All accidents must be reported to the park office.

The climbing environment: The is a no-chalk ethic area; please read page 192 to learn more. The rock is very abrasive, meaning you need to set up anchors carefully and pad slings and ropes as necessary. Tape is good; cams and medium stoppers work well.

The Minnesota Climbing Management Plan: *Climber Registration*—Rock climbing permits will be valid for the calendar year and may be obtained free of charge, in person or by mail, by contacting the park office.

Closures—Climbing is generally allowed within the Carlton Peak area of Temperance River State Park as described in this guidebook. New route development within the described area is allowed within this policy without further permission. Climbers interested in climbing or developing routes outside of these areas or in other parts of the park may request permission in writing through the parts of the park manager. Requests for new routes will be reviewed to determine the appropriateness of the request and the impact on park resources.

Alteration of the Natural Environment—The local climbing ethic at Carlton Peak has been to discourage the use of chalk. Park Management supports this ethic and encourages climbers to support it also.

CARLTON PEAK OVERVIEW

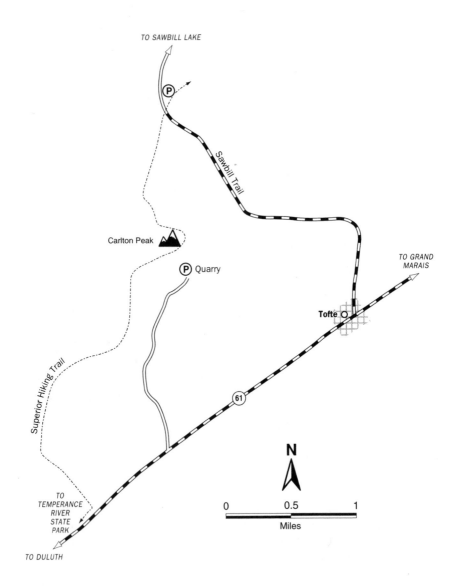

TO SAWBILL LAKE

Sawbill Trail

Carlton Peak

Quarry

Superior Hiking Trail

TO GRAND MARAIS

Tofte

61

N

| 0 | 0.5 | 1 |

Miles

TO TEMPERANCE RIVER STATE PARK

TO DULUTH

NO CHALK AREA

Services: Temperance River State Park is the obvious choice (busy in the summer) for camping during the summer (see Appendix A). See the Superior National Forest map for other options farther inland. There is currently no camping in the quarry area or elsewhere around the base of the summit knob. There is a grocery, gas, restaurants, and an outdoor store (no climbing gear) at Tofte.

Approach: Drive to the town of Tofte and turn North onto the Sawbill Trail (Cook County Road 2). Follow signs to the Britton Peak parking lot, which is 2.6 miles from Minnesota Highway 61. Do not park on the Sawbill Trail/Superior Hiking Trail intersection. The hike from the parking lot to the road takes less than five minutes. Follow the Superior Hiking Trail across the road, then along boardwalks and up to Carlton Peak. This hike takes about 30 minutes while gaining 300 vertical feet. Continue along the base of the summit knob past the intersection with the summit trail and soon reach the first climb (#27). At some point you must leave the Superior Hiking Trail and wade across the gravel at the base to reach the climbs on the left end.

Another approach requires a high-clearance vehicle, especially if the weather has been wet. Cross the Temperance River bridge on MN 61 and continue 0.8 mile to a wide turnoff on the south side of the road with a Superior National Forest sign. A gravel road extends north, toward Carlton Peak. This road is 1.7 miles west of the Sawbill Trail intersection. Take this road north 0.3 mile to the first junction and stay right. Another 0.4 mile takes you past a gated road on the right.

Continue upward as far as you dare. The quarry works have left a lot of deadends, so count on doing a bit of exploring your first time up this way. In general, keep left, aiming for a diamond-shaped rock face, which is part of the old quarry. Find an old road just left of this face and follow it up and right (probably on foot). Park off the road to allow bikes and bigger, badder vehicles to pass.

The summit can be reached via a marked, easy trail that switchbacks hard right. Anything other than easy hiking means you've lost the trail. Approach and setup suggestions are given for a number of routes. Routes are described from left to right (in the opposite direction from which they are encountered).

WEST FACE

To set up the first couple of routes, walk left of *1* to a 20-foot wide, completely vegetated gully. It's about the third possible choice. Hike up this, then cut back right on slabs and dirt (Class 2++) to a bit of a ledge with a tree, or continue to the top to set up routes farther to the right.

1. **#1** (5.6) ★★ Take an inobvious crack left of a scoop and flakes to a small ledge. Setup: The trees are not trustworthy; stoppers and a larger cam or two.

2. **#2** (5.5) ★★ A corner leads to the right end of a ledge. Setup: See previous route.

WEST FACE—LEFT

NO CHALK AREA

WEST FACE—CENTER

WEST FACE—RIGHT

3. **#3** (5.10d) ★★ Thirty feet right of #2 is a thin crack that leads through the right side of an unusual overhang.

4. **#4** (5.7) Up the crack and around the left side of an ear, probably battling a tree or two along the way.

5. **#5** (5.6) Start just right of some blobs of rock and up to overhang.

6. **#6** (5.6) Just right of the previous route.

7. **#7** (5.3) A curving flake just left of #8.

8. **#8** (5.6) ★ Left of #9 is a dark recess with a 5'x 2' block 8' up. Climb the block, and up to a tree.

SOUTH BUTTRESS

Setting up the first few routes may require your rappelling down to a lower ledge. The large corner of #16 is a good landmark. It is a hike to traverse around right and down from the top of #25 to find it.

9. **#9** (5.10c) ★ A crack squirms through small overhangs to a birch.

10. **#10** (5.10d) ★★ Six feet right of #9 is a thin seam. Climb 5', then left and up at your first chance.

11. **#11** (5.7) Just left of #12 is a dirt alcove with several downed trees. A crack ascends the right side of this alcove past a tree. At the overhang, 1) do a moss-fest up the crack on the right side, 2) cut straight right (crux) and then back left, or 3) don't bother. I suggest the last option.

SOUTH BUTTRESS—LEFT

**SOUTH BUTTRESS—
CENTER**

NO CHALK AREA

SOUTH BUTTRESS—RIGHT

12. **#12** (5.10a) ★★★ Start up the left-leaning crack and pull through a pocketed face. Subdue the roof above using handcrack (5.9-). Setup: At right end of line of junipers.

13. **#13** (5.10d) ★★★ A nifty route. Start in a small left-facing corner, then up a left-leaning crack. Traverse right to the crux, a V-groove lacking all the right holds. Setup: Over edge at left end of line of junipers about 30' right of #16.

14. **#14** (5.10d) Start left of #15, then move right to join that route.

15. **#15** (5.11c) ★★ Just left of the #16 corner is a pointed flake on the main wall. From its top, climb the thin crack to the corner and roof above.

16. **#16** (5.8) ★★★ The major right-facing corner. Zip up excellent finger locks to an overhang (watch for loose stuff). Puzzle out the final few moves. A variation (5.9) goes up the thin crack on the left wall, exiting left at the top. Setup: A small corner with trees, just left of a large, downsloping slab with a tree ledge just below and to the right of the slab.

17. **#17** (5.6) Twenty feet right of the large right-facing corner is a shallow groove. Follow the groove to an easy ramp above.

18. **#18** (5.10c) ★ Just left of the chimney formed by the large block is a pointed talus block. Climb up, staying right of the lower trees, to a stance just left of a tree. Move up and left to a small seam.

19. **#19** (5.10+) The major crack inside the chimney on the right wall.

SOUTH FACE

The tops of these routes are most easily reached by hiking up and right from #27 on the Superior Hiking Trail. As the trail levels out, a set of ledges stairsteps up and left (Class 2). Cut left a few yards to a worn area that forms the tops of these climbs.

20. **#20** (5.5) The chimney between the block and the main wall, starting from the outside. Variation: Go up the blunt ridge of the block (5.4?).

21. **#21** (5.5) From the top of the block, go right around the overhang.

22. **#22** (5.7) From the top of the block, go farther right around the overhang.

23. **#23** (5.12a) Right of the huge block is an area with large talus blocks. A stepped overhang lies above. Work up and right around this obstacle to the corner above.

24. **#24** (5.12b) For a harder climb, start the previous route in the right corner.

25. **#25** (5.9) ★★ The small corner right of Route 24 leads to more moderate climbing.

26. **#26** (5.8) ★ Between #25 and #27, go up a flake edge to a dihedral ending just left of a pine tree.

27. **#27** (5.8) ★ About 25' right of a large boulder is a left-leaning finger crack and dihedral. The crux is right off the ground.

NO CHALK AREA

SOUTH FACE

APPENDIX A: CLIMBING SHOPS, ETC.

CLIMBING SHOPS, GUIDE SERVICES, CLIMBING GYMS

Sport Haven (gear)
U.S. Highway 12 & West Highway 33
Baraboo, WI
(608) 356-9218

Midwest Mountaineering (gear)
309 Cedar Avenue South
Minneapolis, MN 55454
(612) 339-3433

Thrifty Outfitters (gear, repair)
309 Cedar Avenue South
Minneapolis, MN 55454
(612) 339-6290

Vertical Endeavors (gym, gear, guide)
844 Arcade Street
St. Paul, MN
(651) 776-1430

P.J. Asch Otterfitters (gym, gear)
413 East Nelson
Stillwater, MN 55082
(651) 430-2286

REI (gear)
1955 West County Road B2
Roseville, MN 55113
(651) 653-0211

REI (gym, gear)
750 West 79th Street
Bloomington, MN 55420
(612) 884-4315

REI (gear)
7483 West Towne Way
Madison, WI 53719

REI (gear)
13100 West Capital Drive
Brookfield, WI 53005

Out-N-About Gear (gear)
47 NE 4th Street
Waite Park, MN 56387
320-251-9036

Eastern Mountain Sports (gear)
915 County Road 42 West
Burnsville, MN 55306
(612) 898-3688

Vertical Stronghold (gym, gear)
719 West Frances Street
Appleton, WI, 54914
(920) 734-0321

Solid Rock Sports (gym, gear)
1034 North 4th Street
Milwaukee, WI
(414) 272-7625

Prairie Walls Climbing Gym (gym, gear)
4420 19th Street NW
Rochester, MN 55901
(507) 292-0511

Footprints Climbing Gym (gym, gear, guide)
9208 James Avenue South, Bay 3
Bloomington, MN 55431
(612) 884-7996

Ski Hut (gear)
1032 East 4th Street
Duluth, MN 55805

Continental Ski Shop (gear)
1305 East First Street
Duluth, MN 55805

On Belay (guide)
9325 Polaris Lane
Maple Grove, MN 55369

Dairyland Expeditions LLC (guide)
719 West Frances Street
Appleton, WI, 54914
(920) 734-0321

Boulders Climbing Gym
3964 Commercial Avenue
Madison, WI 53714
(608) 244-8100

Adventure Rock (gym)
21250 West Capital Drive
Brookfield, WI
(262) 790-6800

Erehwon Mountain Outfitter (gear)
7948 Tree Lane
Madison, WI 53717
(608) 833-9191

Life Tools (gear)
930 Waube Lane
Green Bay, WI 54304
(920) 339-8484

STATE PARKS

General information for all Minnesota state parks, state forests, and scientific and natural areas:
(612) 296-6157 or (800) 657-3929

Minnesota State Park camping reservations:
(612) 922-9000 or (800) 246-2267
TDD (612) 890-2883 or (800) 334-7413

General Information on Wisconsin Tourism:
(800) 432-8747

Wisconsin State Park camping reservations:
(999) 947-2757

Blue Mounds State Park
Route 1, Box 52
Luverne, MN 56156
(507) 283-1307

Jay Cook State Park
500 Highway 210 East
Carlton, MN 55718
(218) 384-4610

Tettegouche State Park
474 Highway 61 East
Silver Bay, MN 55614
(218) 226-6365

Temperance River State Park
Box 33
Schroeder, MN 55613
(218) 663-7476

Interstate State Park (MN)
P.O. Box 254
Taylors Falls, MN 55084
(651) 465-5711

Interstate State Park (WI)
P.O. Box 703
St. Croix Falls, WI 54024
(715) 483-3747

Devil's Lake State Park
South 5975 Park Road
Baraboo, WI 53913
(608) 356-8301

CAMPGROUNDS

Wheeler's Campground
East 11329 Highway 159
Baraboo, WI 53913
920-734-0321

OTHER RESOURCES

Minnesota Travel Information Center
500 Metro Square, 121 7th Place East
Saint Paul, MN 55101-2146
(651) 296-5029
(800) 657-3700
www.exploreminnesota.com

Wisconsin Department of Tourism
201 West Washington Avenue
PO Box 7976
Madison WI 53707-7976
(800) 432-8747
http://travelwisconsin.com

Minnesota Department of Natural Resources
Information Center
500 Lafayette Road
Saint Paul, MN 55155-4040
www.dnr.state.mn.us

Wisconsin Dept. of Natural Resources
101 South Webster
Madison, WI 53703
(608) 266-2621
www.dnr.state.wi.us

Superior National Forest
8901 Grand Avenue Place
Duluth, MN 55808
(218) 626-4300
www.snf.toofarnorth.org

Wisconsin Outdoor Access (WOA)
301 South Bedford Street
Madison, WI 53703
(608) 257-2939
http://climbingcentral.com/WOA/WOA.html

APPENDIX B: SUGGESTED LEADS

Here are some suggested leads. I haven't done them all, and I don't know how good a climber you are. These routes have reasonable protection and are generally nice climbs. They aren't the only good leads at these areas, either. Almost all of the climbs lack bolts, pitons, or other fixed pro. I haven't recommended many harder routes; use your own judgement here. Remember that ratings vary between areas. Limited protection is indicated by an R; X means no protection.

TAYLORS FALLS
5.5	Sonny and Juanita
5.5	Blue Moon
5.5	Rosebush (loose at top)
5.6	Keyhole
5.7	Piece of Cake (very slippery)
5.7	Air Conditioned
5.8	Inside Corner
5.8	Lost Ego
5.10a	Yosemite Crack
5.10a	The Bulge
5.10a	Sentinel Crack

BLUE MOUNDS
5.5	Ivy Right
5.7	Crazy Crack
5.8	Jasper's Dihedral (large pro)
5.9	Jammer
5.10-	Balcony Right (protection difficult)
5.10c	Oath of Fealty (2 or 3 fist or larger cams)

DEVIL'S LAKE
5.4	Queen's Throne
5.5	Boy Scout
5.6-	The Spine (crack only)
5.6	The Pretzel
5.6	Push-Mi Pull-You
5.7	Brinton's Crack
5.7	Berkeley
5.7	Peter's Project
5.8	Birch Tree Crack
5.10a	Upper Diagonal
5.10b/c	Congratulations
5.10b	Cheetah
5.10b	Sometimes Crack
5.11	Thoroughfare

PALISADE HEAD
5.8	Danger High Voltage (large pro)
5.9	Phantom Crack (below the crack is 5.6X)
5.10a	Laceration Jam (5.6R last pitch)

SHOVEL POINT
5.6	Only the Lonely
5.6	The Great Yawn (large pro)
5.6	Out on a Limb
C3/5.12	Great Barrier Roof

MYSTICAL MOUNTAIN ZONE
5.7+	Over the Rainbow
5.10a	Jack Be Nimble (#4 Camalot)

SECTION 13
5.9	Rubble Trouble Direct
5.11a	Digit Damage

CARLTON PEAK
5.5	#2
5.6	#1
5.8	#16

APPENDIX C: THE MINNESOTA CLIMBING MANAGEMENT PLAN

The text below is a copy of the general guidelines of The Minnesota Climbing Management Plan. I have omitted the definitions section. Specific management criteria for each park are presented in the appropriate chapter. Please note that by default, it is illegal to rock climb in Minnesota state parks unless permission has been granted. Keep this in mind if you are scoping out new areas.

Purpose: To provide a framework for the management of rock climbing in Minnesota State Parks, so it is done in a manner that provides for the safety of all users, minimizes conflicts with other types of use and allows for the protection of the resources. These guidelines are intended to acknowledge the use of certain sites within the state park system as permissible rock climbing areas, in so far as the park's natural and cultural resources are not being irrevocably altered, and clarify a permitting system for their use.

Policy statement: Rock climbing guidelines for State Parks are based on the recognition that 1) rock climbing is an established recreational activity in Minnesota State Parks; 2) providing areas for rock climbing in Minnesota State Parks is consistent with our mission to provide appropriate recreational opportunities; and 3) the increased popularity of rock climbing has created the need for the Department of Natural Resources, Division of Parks and Recreation to develop guidelines to manage the activity and its impact on park resources.

Management guidelines: Rock climbing is allowed on natural rock faces at the following parks: Blue Mounds, Interstate, Tettegouche, and Temperance River. Some areas within these parks may be restricted or closed to climbing because of concerns about the safety of other park users, potential impacts to park resources and values, or other park management concerns (See "Closures").

Developing new areas for climbing or climbing in non-designated parks will be permitted only after management approval through an identified process. Climbers interested in developing routes outside of defined areas or in other parts of the park may request permission in writing through the park manager. Requests for new routes will be reviewed to determine the appropriateness of the request and impact on the resources.

Approval or disapproval will be based on resource management, compatibility with other uses, aesthetics, access, or other similar management concerns and will not be an endorsement of the safety of the routes which may be used. Choice of routes, types, and use of equipment and other issues related to the safety of climbers will always be the climber's responsibility.

SPECIFIC GUIDELINES
Climbing permits
A. *Climbing areas restricted.* All cliffs, rock faces, and other park areas suitable for climbing are designated restricted areas under Minn. Rules 6100.2100. They are also subject to protection under Minn. Rules 6100.0900.

These areas are closed to all kinds of rock climbing, but may be opened to climbing by special use (climbing) permits, issued to individuals or commercial groups and shall be so identified. These guidelines restrict these areas only for climbing. They may be open for other uses in accordance with Minn. Rules 6100.2000, subp. 1, and park procedures.

B. *Permit required.* No person may rock climb in any restricted area without first obtaining a special use (climbing) permit from the park manager.

C. *Special use permits for climbers.* Special use permits for climbers ("climbing permits") shall be issued annually and shall expire at the end of the calendar year. Climbing permits shall be issued upon request during regular business hours at the park office (or through the mail by writing the park office), and are valid only for the park where issued. Climbing permits may contain restrictions to avoid environmental damage, overuse, pre-emption of climbing areas, or displacement of other park users. No fee shall be charged for climbing permits.

D. *Special use permits for commercial operators.* Commercial enterprises such as schools, universities, businesses and other organizations, individuals and entities that provide instruction or guiding services for rock climbers in state parks must first obtain a special use permit for commercial climbing ("commercial climbing permit"). Commercial climbing permits shall be issued for a specific date or series of dates, and shall specify the location where climbing is authorized and the number of individuals that may be included in the group. In addition to the commercial climbing permit, all individual climbers, instructors and guides each have their own climbing permit. Commercial climbing permits may contain restrictions or limitations on the number issued in order to avoid environmental damage, overuse, pre-emption of climbing areas, or displacement of other park users.

E. *Insurance.* Commercial climbing permittees are required to furnish a certificate of insurance valid for the effective dates of the permit, listing the State of Minnesota as a named insured. The amount of coverage shall be at least as much as the state's limits of liability under the Minnesota Tort Claims Act, Minn. Stat. §3.736. As of May 1995, these limits are $200,000 per individual and $600,000 per incident.

F. *Warning and liability disclaimer.* Rock climbing is an inherently dangerous activity. All persons are strongly urged to seek competent instruction and develop appropriate skill before climbing on their own. The State of Minnesota does not certify climbers, instructors or guides, or otherwise determine their qualifications. Nor does the state rate climbing locations, routes or conditions, or determine their safety.

Note: The State of Minnesota is not liable if a climber gets hurt or killed while climbing in Minnesota State Parks. If climbers choose to climb, they do so at their own risk!

Information and education: Park management will work with the climbing community to develop information and education materials which foster an environmental climbing ethic. Information kiosks or bulletin boards may be developed near climbing areas to provide a communication link between climbers and park management.

Climber Advisory Committee: State Parks will form a climbing advisory group made up of representatives of the climbing community to advise park management on climbing issues. Each park is encouraged to include climbers in park advisory groups to provide input to park management on climbing issues.

Closures: Even with the appropriate permit for rock climbing, some areas may be closed to that use. Rock climbing may not be allowed where it creates a conflict with vehicular use of roads or designated use of trails (i.e., hiking). Climbing areas may also be closed based on other conflicts of use, where allowing climbing may endanger other park users, or for significant aesthetic concerns. Areas closed to all general public use are also closed to climbing.

Areas may be closed, or restrictions may be placed on climbing, to protect natural resources such as: nesting raptors; endangered or sensitive wildlife, plants or habitats; cultural resources; or to protect sensitive geologic features.

Closures or restrictions may be placed on climbing to prevent conflicts with adjoining land uses or with the owners of adjacent property.

Climbing on manmade structures (i.e., buildings and towers) or using manmade structures (i.e., fences or railings) for protection is prohibited. In areas where manmade structures have traditionally been used for protection, consideration will be given to installing appropriate permanent protection, as appropriate under this policy.

Areas opened/closed to climbing within each park will be identified and will be mapped and signed at appropriate locations within the park.

Secondary impacts of rock climbing, such as volunteer trails on cliff top and bottom areas will be addressed when necessary to minimize impacts on the park resources. Closure of a route to climbing may be used to address secondary impacts, but if other effective and practicable solutions can be cost effective, they will be considered prior to closures.

Use of climbing protection: Minnesota State Parks strongly endorse a "clean climbing" philosophy. In all but very limited, pre-approved instances, placement of hardware will be limited to that which can be temporarily placed using the climber's fingers. All such protection must be placed and removed without altering the rock.

In some locations and situations within Minnesota State Parks, fixed anchors (or protection) have been installed by climbers for the purpose of climber safety and to minimize climber impacts on natural resources.

Existing fixed protection will be documented and evaluated through the assistance of the climbing community. In general, existing fixed protection in place as of March 1, 1995, will be permitted to remain in place. In situations where fixed protection creates a visual conflict with other park users or impact on the natural resources, the fixed anchors may require camouflaging or removal. Slings or other visually distracting hardware shall not be left in place on fixed anchors. Where existing fixed protection is found by climbers to be unsound, it may be removed, if possible. Replacement may be allowed upon review by park management and members of the climbing advisory committee.

Note: Decisions to allow placement or replacement of fixed protection will be based on aesthetic, resource protection, and other park management concerns.

Minnesota State Parks will not permit proliferation of bolting and bolted routes. In very limited instances, where fixed anchors are needed for protection of adjacent resources or as alternatives to present tie-off points, they may be approved. New fixed anchors (after March 1, 1995) may not be installed without the approval of the Division of Parks and Recreation. An application form for fixed anchor placement will be available at park offices. Applications will be evaluated by park management and the climbing advisory committee. The Division of Parks and Recreation has the final word in approving or rejecting any fixed anchor applications.

All approved fixed anchors must be commercially manufactured for climbing fall protection and must be installed according to manufacturer's specifications and only with the approval of the Division of Parks and Recreation. All approved permanent anchors will be documented in park files. Any fixed anchors placed without park management permission are a violation of park rules.

Note: The decision to climb a route whether fixed anchors have been placed or not allowed, and the decision to utilize any existing fixed anchor are based on climber judgement. State Parks are not responsible for costs, condition, or for appropriate and safe placement of new fixed anchors or for the maintenance and condition of existing fixed protection, and the use thereof is not endorsed by State Parks.

Climber safety and emergency procedures: Rock climbing is recognized to be a form of "risk recreation" with potential hazards to those involved in it. State Parks strongly advocate that the safest possible climbing practices be used for all climbing in State Parks, but can assume no responsibility for climbers safety. Climbers are solely responsible for their safety while climbing, and for the safety of others who may be affected by their actions.

Rock quarries, and other rock areas which have been altered and affected by human activity, shall be signed at primary access points. The signing is intended to alert climbers of the former activity at the site, so they are better able to make their decisions on climbing in the area.

Climber equipment and activities must not interfere with the safety of, or use of the park, by others.

State parks shall not accept responsibility for providing rescue services to climbers. Each park will work with local rescue squads to be knowledgeable about available emergency rescue services related to rock climbing incidents. The location of the nearest pay phone, emergency facilities, and emergency phone numbers will be posted at prominent climbing areas or at park offices, and will be included in written materials provided to climbers. They will also be indicated in the park-specific rock climbing management plan. All injuries are to be reported to the park office.

Unattended equipment: The use of unattended equipment to reserve climbing routes is prohibited unless allowed by a Special-use Permit issued by the Division of Parks and Recreation. If such use creates conflicts for other park users, and park management is unable to resolve the problem through other means, the equipment may be removed in order to allow others to use the climbing route or adjacent facilities.

Alteration of the natural environment: Activities which alter the natural environment (i.e., chipping or gluing of natural or artificial holds, "trundling" of rock, or "gardening") are prohibited.

In some circumstances, climbing activities may cause temporary visual impacts offensive to other park users. Initial efforts to limit the visual impacts (i.e., chalk) will be through climber education. Other management actions may be taken if climber education efforts are unsuccessful.

Support facilities: The need for support facilities (i.e., parking areas, toilets, trash cans etc.) for climbing areas will be determined on a location by location basis.

Policy changes: Normal policy review will be done annually by a group made up of park management, resource specialists and members of the climbers' advisory committees. Policy revisions will be incorporated into a draft proposal and sent to registered climbers for comment and review prior to implementation.

Timeline: All comments shall be submitted in writing to:
Department of Natural Resources
Minnesota State Parks
Operations Manager
500 Lafayette Road
Saint Paul, MN 55155-4039

Comments must be received by November 1 of each year for consideration. Policy revisions, if necessary, will be incorporated into a draft proposal and sent out for review by January 1. A final policy will be implemented by April 1 of each year.

In the event park management identifies a need to implement a policy change outside of the above timeline, the timeline may by waived. Park management will work with the climbing advisory committee and seek appropriate input when time permits.

Any alterations in policy or in park-specific rock climbing management plans will be posted at the climbing information sites or provided in written materials provided to climbers as far in advance as possible.

Additions of new climbing areas in parks: New climbing areas in parks may be permitted upon addition to this policy. Submittals shall be incorporated based on assessment of the aforementioned issues and only after completion of a rock climbing management plan for the unit.

INDEX

SYMBOLS

A

B

ABOUT THE AUTHOR

Mike Farris is an Associate Professor of Biology and past director of the Environmental Studies program at Hamline University in St. Paul, Minnesota. Since 1975, he has climbed rock, ice, and alpine routes in the US, Canada, and Mexico. As a plant ecologist he has done research on cliff vegetation and has worked with land managers to preserve both climbing access and cliff ecosystems. When he's not climbing he enjoys running and has completed several 100-mile trail races. Since 1985 he has lived in Minnesota with his wife Kathleen and son David.

ACCESS: It's every climber's concern

The Access Fund, a national, non-profit climbers' organization, works to keep climbing areas open and to conserve the climbing environment. Need help with closures? land acquisition? legal or land management issues? funding for trails and other projects? starting a local climbers' group? CALL US!

Climbers can help preserve access by being committed to leaving the environment in its natural state. Here are some simple guidelines:

• **STRIVE FOR ZERO IMPACT** especially in environmentally sensitive areas like caves. Chalk can be a significant impact on dark and porous rock—don't use it around historic rock art. Pick up litter, and leave trees and plants intact.

• **DISPOSE OF HUMAN WASTE PROPERLY** Use toilets whenever possible. If toilets are not available, dig a "cat hole" at least six inches deep and 200 feet from any water, trails, campsites, or the base of climbs. *Always pack out toilet paper.* On big wall routes, use a "poop tube" and carry waste up and off with you (the old "bag toss" is now illegal in many areas).

• **USE EXISTING TRAILS** Cutting switchbacks causes erosion. When walking off-trail, tread lightly, especially in the desert where cryptogamic soils (usually a dark crust) take thousands of years to form and are easily damaged. Be aware that "rim ecologies" (the clifftop) are often highly sensitive to disturbance.

• **BE DISCREET WITH FIXED ANCHORS** *Bolts are controversial and are not a convenience*—don't place 'em unless they are *really* necessary. Camouflage all anchors. Remove unsightly slings from rappel stations (better to use steel chain or welded cold shuts). Bolts sometimes can be used pro-actively to protect fragile resources—consult with your local land manager.

• **RESPECT THE RULES** and speak up when other climbers don't. Expect restrictions in designated wilderness areas, rock art sites, caves, and to protect wildlife, especially nesting birds of prey. *Power drills are illegal in wilderness and all national parks.*

• **PARK AND CAMP IN DESIGNATED AREAS** Some climbing areas require a permit for overnight camping.

• **MAINTAIN A LOW PROFILE** Leave the boom box and day-glo clothing at home—the less climbers are heard and seen, the better.

• **RESPECT PRIVATE PROPERTY** Be courteous to land owners. Don't climb where you're not wanted.

• **JOIN THE ACCESS FUND!** To become a member, make a tax-deductible donation of $25 or more.

The Access Fund

Preserving America's Diverse Climbing Resources
PO Box 17010 Boulder, CO 80308
303.545.6772 • www.accessfund.org